FUN
IS
GOOD

FUN IS GOOD

How to Create Joy & Passion in Your Workplace & Career

Mike Veeck
& Pete Williams

Advantage®

Published by Advantage, Charleston, South Carolina.
Member of Advantage Media Group.

ADVANTAGE is a registered trademark and the Advantage colophon is a trademark of Advantage Media Group, Inc.

Printed in the United States of America.

ISBN: 978-159932-334-3
LCCN: 2012934980

This publication is designed to provide accurate and authoritative information in regard to the subject matter covered. It is sold with the understanding that the publisher is not engaged in rendering legal, accounting, or other professional services. If legal advice or other expert assistance is required, the services of a competent professional person should be sought.

Advantage Media Group is proud to be a part of the Tree Neutral® program. Tree Neutral offsets the number of trees consumed in the production and printing of this book by taking proactive steps such as planting trees in direct proportion to the number of trees used to print books. To learn more about Tree Neutral, please visit www.treeneutral.com. To learn more about Advantage's commitment to being a responsible steward of the environment, please visit www.advantagefamily.com/green

Advantage Media Group is a leading publisher of business, motivation, and self-help authors. Do you have a manuscript or book idea that you would like to have considered for publication? Please visit www.amgbook.com or call 1.866.775.1696

For
Libby, Rebecca & Night Train

Table of Contents

Acknowledgements

THOUGH MY NAME is on the front of this book, "Fun Is Good" is a team effort, a philosophy fine-tuned over the years with input from thousands of people. To list everyone by name would fill up the largest baseball park and then some, but I wanted to single out the following:

To Marv Goldklang, thanks for taking a chance. As I got to know you, I realized that you love taking chances.

To my friends, colleagues, and extended family of the Goldklang Group, thank you for making every day fun. To the fans of our baseball teams, thank you for continually challenging us to make "Fun Is Good" better.

To my coconspirators, Pete Williams and David Black, thank you for making this book a reality. To Amy Rhodes, Jeremy Katz, Pete Fornatale, Sarah Dunn, and the entire team at Rodale, thanks for helping me bring my message to others.

To Libby, thank you for making me laugh; Night Train, thank you for introducing me to the joys of unconditional love; Rebecca, thanks for showing me the meaning of courage.

To Bird Dog, thank you for teaching me about friendship; I'm forever grateful.

To my friend Bill, thanks for daring me to dream; I can't say enough. What an incredible Cinderella story.

To Van, thank you for mentioning me to Roland Hemond.

To Mom, Dad, Marya, Greg, Lisa, Julie, and Chris, thanks for a wonderful fun trip.

And did I mention Libby?

Finally, thanks to Laurie Burnham, Tom Whaley, and Andy Nelson, without whose friendship, life would not be nearly as much fun.

Introduction

FUN IS GOOD.

Most people would agree with this statement. Kids live by this motto. Adults say they do. Corporate executives claim to, though it's mostly lip service.

Companies spend a lot of time writing mission statements, in which they talk about "strategic initiatives" and use big words like "facilitate" and "implement," presumably so they can add "shareholder value."

I suppose a mission statement allows some people to focus better, though what they're focusing on, I'm not sure. I run six minor league baseball teams and for each of them we've drafted a business plan that begins with three simple words:

Fun Is Good.

It's really that simple. Our philosophy begins and ends with the notion that fun is good. That applies to not only the product we're selling—a family-oriented evening at the ballpark full of laughter, zany promotions, wacky stunts, and free giveaways—but also our office environment. We have fun at work. We enjoy what we do, and that rubs off on our customers, who leave our ballparks not only entertained but feeling good about themselves and our product.

Fun Is Good works. We've used the philosophy to transform a half-dozen money-losing or start-up teams into a combined $20 to $30 million business.

Let me take you inside one of our ballparks. It's a balmy summer night in St. Paul, Minnesota, and more than 6,300 people are on hand at Midway Stadium, an ancient concrete slab that we've transformed into a cozy, inviting place with murals, flowers, and laughter. Fans pack the parking lot 3 hours before the game to tailgate, and the air smells of bratwurst, charcoal, and beer. Throughout the game, trains run just 20 feet behind the outfield wall.

As game time approaches, fans drift toward the turnstiles, where a band always plays and there's almost always a free giveaway. Signs are posted prohibiting neckties and "the wave." Sometimes we even hand out freshly baked cookies.

Inside, the official mascot of the St. Paul Saints (a pig) delivers the game ball to the umpires. A 9-year-old public address announcer greets the crowd. In center field, a dozen elaborately costumed "ushertainers" step out from behind the wall and stride toward home plate. Meanwhile, in the stands above third base, a nun gives massages to fans. Along the first base line, kids squeal as they romp through giant inflatable obstacle courses. We sell hot dogs for $1.50, beers for $2. Tickets range from $3 to $8.

During the game, we have a contest or promotion after every half-inning. We have fans sumo wrestle in giant inflatable suits. Instead of having a grounds crew drag the infield in the middle of the game, we have guys *in* drag rake the dirt.

Our teams stage major promotions every night. Perhaps you've heard of some of them. One time, another of our teams, the Charleston RiverDogs, decided to set the all-time *lowest* attendance record and did not allow anyone inside the ballpark. In St. Paul, we gave out inflatable baseball bats emblazoned "Viagra" (though admittedly the folks at Pfizer did not approve). We once hired mimes to stand atop the first base dugout and reenact close plays, only to have the performers pelted with hundreds of hot dogs. For Call in Sick Day, fans cut work and we faxed in excuses to their bosses. Another time, we were thwarted in an attempt to give away a free vasectomy on Father's Day. The Catholic Church, you might say, snipped that one.

The magic continues after the game, long after the fans have departed. About an hour after the last out, someone will pull a keg out from behind one of the concession stands in the concourse. Before long, a couple dozen employees, most of whom have been on the job 15 hours already, will kick back for an hour or so. From interns to executives, they'll replay the day and enjoy one another's company before finally heading home.

I don't imagine this happens in too many workplaces. Most people hate spending even 8 hours with their coworkers and have no interest in learning anything about them, let alone socializing after hours. There's an atmosphere of distrust between managers and employees— if there's any emotion in the office at all. Most workplaces seem like prisons, with people walking around like zombies, passing time until they're free to go home.

Somehow, in our haste to seize the American dream, we've sucked the fun, passion, and creativity out of the workplace. Somewhere between kindergarten and our 20s we lost that sense of joy and wonder. We've forgotten that the way you make a living is directly connected to your soul.

Fun is good. It's a basic human need. Life is too short to spend 40 to 80 hours a week in an unpleasant situation. Maybe you hate your job. You rationalize it by saying, "I love my home life, my family, and my hobbies." I can appreciate that. But I don't want to love just part of my life; I want to love my entire life, and I want my employees to feel the same way.

I know what you're thinking, Mr. Middle Manager. "I don't have the luxury of getting to know my employees. I have the bottom line to look after. I provide my workers with salary and health insurance. I can't worry about their personal fulfillment."

Oh no? Think about what happens over time if you fail to address what Bruce Springsteen calls "the human touch." You'll endure lost productivity and employee turnover. They'll go to other companies that subscribe to the Fun Is Good philosophy and end up kicking your butt.

Meanwhile, at your place, customer service suffers because employees don't care about the company. Business will go elsewhere. Then there are your customers, at least the few you have left. Professional sports takes a lot of criticism, and rightly so, for treating its customers—the fans—poorly. Instead of striving to serve their customers better, they've adopted this warped sense of entitlement where they take business for granted. Yet most corporations are no different. They don't listen to the people paying their bills.

Customer service, the lifeblood of any business, has become a lost art, in large part because we've forgotten how to have fun at work. If you're not having fun, it's nearly impossible to project the upbeat, positive attitude necessary to serve clients effectively.

Our customers—baseball fans—always ask how our employees manage to look like they're having so much fun around the ballpark during games. The answer is simple: because they are. We're not actors, gathering in the bowels of the stadium beforehand for a pep talk and to put on our "game faces." It's impossible to turn it on and off like that. Customers can spot insincerity.

In the world of minor league baseball, people perform numerous jobs. By the time the game rolls around, most employees already have worked 10-hour days. I don't care how good an actor you are—and we have a few former professional thespians in our organization—

there's no way you could project the Fun Is Good mentality late into the evening if you're not actually having a good time.

I don't imagine you're called upon to work 15-hour days on a regular basis or that you ask your employees to do so. But wouldn't it be nice to think that you not only wouldn't mind doing so but also would enjoy it?

Now, you might think it's all easy if you work in baseball. Who wouldn't have fun?

You think? During the day, we're like any other office. We have sales and marketing and accounting. We have paperwork and file cabinets. Unlike many companies, we have a much smaller staff so everyone has to pitch in on odd jobs and cleaning, which is no small task in that we're also responsible for operating stadiums. Even though we come in at 9 a.m., we hang around until midnight on game nights, which can be up to 70 evenings a year.

We love what we do, and that's what makes it easy. If we can maintain this fun and energy level over the course of a long baseball season, I'm confident you can pull it off in your workplace for the "mere" 8 to 10 hours a day you're there.

Fun isn't just good; it's a necessity. For the last decade, I've shown hundreds of people how to pursue fulfilling careers where they not only grow and thrive but also have fun along the way. I've lectured to dozens of companies on how to boost sales, raise productivity, and improve customer service by introducing this concept to the workplace.

I've received a lot of press for crazy promotions and stunts. (Admittedly, I've often shamelessly courted such publicity.) But behind these cheap theatrics is a sound philosophy that applies to any business.

You don't have to own a baseball team to benefit from Fun Is Good. In fact, anyone who gauges the business success of our baseball teams by our promotions is missing the point. After all, everyone in minor league baseball relies on cheap theatrics because we have no big-name ballplayers to promote.

What makes us successful—and what I would argue makes any company successful—is not necessarily a superior product. (Heck, we have an inherently inferior product: minor league and independent league baseball.) But we succeed on a level where our bigger, well-heeled brethren in the major leagues do not. We do so by providing superior customer service and creating fun in the workplace.

It's a simple formula, but one applied not nearly enough in American business. In this book, I'll show you how to make it work for your career and in your workplace.

The reason I decided to write this book is that there are too many people leading lives that are not as fulfilling as they could be. On one level, I'm thankful for that because it's good for business; people come out to the ballpark to escape and have some much-needed fun. It might be the only time all week they laugh. James Earl Jones got it right in the movie *Field of Dreams* when he lectured Kevin Costner's character on why people would come to watch baseball in his Iowa cornfield:

"People will come, Ray . . . for it is money they have and peace they lack."

Doesn't that last sentence pretty much sum up our American culture? We have money but lack peace in our lives.

Actually, we don't have nearly as much money as we could because we're lacking this fun. Whoever first said that you need to "follow your heart and the money will follow" got it half right. You have to follow the people who are having fun, and then the money will follow.

In this book, you'll see how just a few people with the Fun Is Good attitude can infect an entire workplace. If you're a manager, you'll learn how to find those people. If you want to be one of those people, you'll find out how.

That's an important distinction. I hope managers and business owners have picked up this book, but odds are you're someone lower on the corporate ladder. I'm especially happy to share Fun Is Good with you.

Unlike my dad, who always managed to parlay a modest investment into a controlling position in every business he operated, I've always had to report to someone. Wherever I've gone, I've had to convince someone to give this idea a shot. I've worked in Major League Baseball, which is full of some of the stuffiest, most humorless people you'll ever meet. So I know where the challenge lies.

Businesses are not nearly as prosperous as they could be because they're missing a culture where fun is good, where creativity and irreverence are valued, and where it's okay to take your job, but not yourself, seriously.

We've stopped celebrating in the American workplace. I don't mean birthdays, where employees trudge off to the conference room for a sliver of cake while the boss makes a halfhearted attempt to toast the guest of honor, who would rather be spending the day anywhere but in the office.

Why don't we make a fuss over things truly worth celebrating? There's not a company anywhere that doesn't need to motivate a sales force. Yet they routinely pass over the best, easiest opportunities to do so. In most offices, a salesperson makes a huge sale or lands a big account and the boss says, "That's great. What else you got?"

Most organizations don't take the time to say "thank you." The cynics will say the employee should be happy just to have a job with benefits, especially in tough economic times, especially with employee health care costs soaring, and blah, blah, blah. Now we have to give them a pat on the back?

Why not? Instead of asking, "What else you got?" why not shut everything down for the afternoon and go celebrate at the nearest saloon? Heck, in the world of minor league baseball, if we sell a $25,000 sponsorship package, we're liable not to be seen for 3 days. We don't just reward top salespeople with bonuses; we give them additional days off. They know they are appreciated.

In Detroit, where I spent 2 years working with the Tigers marketing department, we once sold 20,000 full-price tickets to the United Auto Workers. This was during the 2003 season, when the Tigers were trying not to post the worst record in baseball history. This was worthy of not only a celebration but also a press release. Since the media is constantly starved for news, a news outlet picked it up and the employees involved in the sale felt even better about the accomplishment.

Fun Is Good isn't meant to be altruistic, though it's nice to be nice and it's a lot more fun to work somewhere where people are enjoying themselves. Fun Is Good is simply sound business. Our salespeople not only feel appreciated, they come back even more motivated to sell because of the rewards—both tangible and intangible—and also because they feel more a part of the company.

When that attitude infects your entire organization, look out. When people pick up the phones laughing, when they greet customers as if they're trying to let them in on an inside joke, you've created a culture where the best people will want to work and customers will want to spend dollars.

People will come. For it is money they have—and peace they lack.

I'm one of nine children. My father, Bill Veeck, was a huge baseball fan. When the designated hitter rule was adopted, Mom almost left town.

My family's involvement in baseball and the Fun Is Good experience goes back nearly a century.

In 1917, when Dad was 3 years old, his father, sportswriter William Veeck Sr., became president of the Chicago Cubs. By the time Dad was 11, he was working as a vendor, office boy, ticket seller, and groundskeeper. When his father died in 1933, Dad left college to work for the Cubs, eventually becoming club treasurer.

From 1941 until 1981, Dad owned and operated baseball teams—first a minor league franchise in Milwaukee, and then major league clubs in Cleveland, St. Louis, and Chicago. I literally lived at the ballpark as a toddler because my parents had converted office space into an apartment at Sportsman's Park, home of the St. Louis Browns (now the Baltimore Orioles).

Though I'm not sure Dad ever used the phrase, he lived the Fun Is Good philosophy every day of his life.

It wasn't just that he came up with outrageous promotions and stunts, like sending midget Eddie Gaedel up to bat for the Browns. Everything he did was geared toward injecting fun into business, making fans laugh, and serving customers better.

Ever wonder why players have their names on the backs of their uniforms? It's because a lady once suggested to Dad that it would help better identify the players. Back then, before television and nightly sports highlights, players were not as recognizable. Not everyone could afford a program.

Dad was the first to popularize ballpark giveaways, no matter how outrageous, and staged special nights for every ethnic group imaginable. He introduced exploding scoreboards, popularized postgame fireworks, and provided nurseries at the ballpark for children. He handed out roses to ladies as they entered the ballpark and installed full-length mirrors in their rest rooms. He so believed in the concept of customers participating in the fun that he once staged "Grandstand Managers Day," where fans called the plays by flashing placards.

Dad once acquired a copy of a recording of Harry Caray singing "Take Me Out to the Ball Game" during the seventh-inning stretch in the broadcast booth at Chicago's Comiskey Park. Apparently our broadcast network had secretly taped Harry singing along to the organist between innings, and Dad threatened to play it over the loudspeakers. Instead, Harry started singing live, starting a singalong tradition that Harry later took across town to Wrigley Field and the Cubs.

Dad's promotions and stunts were considered lowbrow by the uptight bluebloods who ran major league baseball, who, like their corporate successors today, believed the product should sell itself and that there's no need to cater to the customer by introducing anything that could be considered fun into the game. They continually tried to run Dad out of the game for being progressive and innovative and making them look bad by drawing more fans with superior customer service.

Few organizations operate with more self-entitlement than Major League Baseball. Is it any wonder that its fan base and television ratings continue to erode? MLB once was considered the national pastime, a title that now belongs to the NFL or perhaps NASCAR.

When Dad died in 1986, we had him cremated so he wouldn't constantly be rolling in his grave. With the way baseball operates, he'd never get any rest.

Dad was a champion of the little guy, which incidentally is the last line on his plaque in the Baseball Hall of Fame. He roamed the stands during games, took the pulse of the city by constantly visiting saloons, and was a tireless public speaker, talking to any group no matter the size of the audience.

Dad was ahead of his time when it came to managing people and running a business. He sought input from everyone, answered his own phones, and never had an unlisted home number. Hirings and firings often took place at the bar over beers. He took the doors off the offices, which many people assumed was to foster an open-door policy. It was, but Dad also recognized that employees grow suspicious when they see colleagues meeting behind closed doors.

He wasn't just the champion of the little guy: He *was* the little guy. Dad was among the last men to own a major professional sports franchise not having made a fortune in another business. The creative financing he put together to purchase teams was legendary, and the reason he had to outwork and outhustle his wealthier competitors was that it was the only way he could stay solvent. He couldn't write off losses against other businesses.

Wherever he went, he brought fun to the ballpark. Attendance soared, and often the teams improved. In 1948, the Cleveland Indians won the World Series and drew 2.6 million fans, a big league record that the Tribe didn't top until 1995 after they had built a new stadium. Even the New York Yankees didn't draw more at home until 1998.

Back in Dad's time, the owner took a far more active role in player acquisition than owners do today, and it's worth noting that the Indians haven't won a World Series since 1948. The Chicago White Sox haven't been back to the World Series since 1959, the first year of Dad's tenure on the South Side.

Like many sons, I had no intention of getting into the family business. After spending much of my childhood in trouble, I got my act together long enough to graduate in 1972 from Loyola College in Baltimore. I put my B.A. in English to immediate use by spending 150 of the next 156 weeks in motel lounges, drumming and playing guitar with various rock-and-roll bands, including one known as Chattanooga Glass.

We opened each evening with a Bob Dylan song. It was called "You Ain't Goin' Nowhere." And I wasn't.

During a swing through Easton, Maryland, our home for much of the 1960s and early '70s, Dad and I had lunch. In our family, lunch meant a daylong visit to a local saloon, drinking beer from 11 o'clock on. He mentioned that he was about to acquire the White Sox for a second time and, after about 12 hours of discussion over lunch, he convinced me to come to work with him.

Dad insisted I start at the bottom, just as he had. Within a year, I found a niche staging rock concerts at the ballpark. The revenues from the AC/DC, Aerosmith, and Eagles concerts we put on at Comiskey helped defray the rising salaries of our players.

The beginning of the end of Dad's tenure in baseball came on July 12, 1979, and I'm partly to blame. Then 28, I thought it would be a great idea to capitalize on the antidisco fervor sweeping the nation. Fans were instructed to bring a disco record to Comiskey Park, and we were going to blow them up on the field in a dumpster between games of a doubleheader against the Detroit Tigers as part of "Disco Demolition Night."

More than 100,000 people showed up, twice the ballpark capacity. Many of them stormed the field when the records were destroyed. The umpires ruled the surface unplayable, and the White Sox had to forfeit the second game.

Dad and I were ripped mercilessly by the media. "Riot at Comiskey," screamed the *Chicago Sun-Times*. The *Chicago Tribune* proclaimed it a disgrace. The promotion was deemed the worst in baseball history. Bowie Kuhn, the commissioner of baseball, issued an edict banning "negative promotions."

I was inconsolable, though Dad did his best. "The promotion worked too well," he said.

By then, Dad's health was declining, and free agency was making it difficult for the noncorporate owner to compete financially. Fewer than 18 months later he sold the White Sox.

Between Disco Demolition and my family's antiestablishment ways, I was effectively blackballed from baseball. I dealt with it by drinking, which led to the end of my first marriage and caused me to lose custody of my son, William, known to all as "Night Train." I drifted to Florida, where I hung drywall, worked in a jai alai fronton, and drank heavily as I pondered the failure of Disco Demolition Night and my lost baseball career.

I tried Alcoholics Anonymous, but what I really needed to survive was the temple of baseball. My life was a mess, and the thing I love about baseball is that it's all about renewal and second chances. I went to work in advertising, eventually starting my own agency, while continuing to write letters to every team in organized baseball looking for work.

In 1989, I got my break. Roland Hemond, Dad's former general manager from the White Sox, ran into Van Schley, a documentary filmmaker who owned several minor league teams and was looking for someone to run the Miami Miracle, an unaffiliated minor league outfit drawing only a few hundred fans.

"I need someone like Bill Veeck," Schley said.

Dad was gone by then, but Roland explained that I was available.

Schley's partners included actor Bill Murray and singer Jimmy Buffett. Another one of their partners, Marv Goldklang, called and offered me a job for $25,000 running the Miracle.

So I took Fun Is Good back to the minors, where it had begun more than 40 years earlier in Milwaukee with Dad. Over the next 9 years, I helped the Goldklang Group build a minor league empire of profitable teams, all widely acclaimed for their customer service and bringing baseball back to the fans.

We did it by being creative and having fun. Bill Murray donned a uniform and served as the first base coach. Ila Borders took the mound in St. Paul as the first modern-day female professional baseball player. We held all-night movie parties and ballpark concerts. Kids ran the bases after games, worked the public address system during games, and made themselves at home.

By the mid-1990s, I was starting to get feelers from Major League Baseball teams. The Minnesota Twins, begrudgingly acknowledging the success of the Saints down the road, brought me in for an interview but never offered a job. The Florida Marlins did offer a gig, but it wasn't the right fit for either of us.

In 1998, Vince Naimoli ended my two-decade exile from Major League Baseball by hiring me as senior vice president of sales and marketing for the Tampa Bay Devil Rays, a team that had just finished a disappointing inaugural season at the box office. Finally, Fun Is Good was coming back to the big leagues.

The Rays, as a business, had a reputation for being stuffy and anything but fan-friendly. So I scheduled a full slate of promotions for 1999 and introduced a marketing campaign called "Off the Wall," featuring irreverent ads that showed that the franchise had a sense of humor. We scheduled "Labor Day," in which pregnant women got in for free, and "Conversion Day," in which local Yankee fans could redeem their caps for Devil Rays headgear.

It never took off. Perhaps it was doomed from my first meeting with Devil Rays executives, when I introduced myself by spinning a top on the conference room table. I got nothing but puzzled looks—not even a smile.

Over the next 7 months, I learned that the uptight baseball culture Dad had battled for years had grown even more corporate. It's hard to be "Off the Wall" when nobody in the office is off the wall. It's a tough thing to fake. You can learn to be off the wall, but for the most part this was not a group willing to learn.

My frustration came to a head when I arrived home after a day of office politics and had the nerve to vent to my wife, Libby. She had her hands full dealing with our daughter, Rebecca, who recently had been diagnosed with retinitis pigmentosa, a horrible disease that causes blindness. Libby wondered where my priorities were.

My resignation followed the next day, though I probably would have been fired before long. Some might say Major League Baseball is beyond hope when it comes to the Veeck family and Fun Is Good; I disagree. In 2001, I went to work for the Florida Marlins as a marketing consultant, reporting to team president Dave Dombrowski. Dave's first job was working for Dad in Chicago; I hired him, in fact. When Dave took a similar position with the Tigers, I followed.

Dave gets Fun Is Good. Still, we must deal with a baseball culture that takes its business, such as it is, for granted. I fought the battle with Dave from Detroit for 2 years before I departed, and slowly we made inroads. I know if we can bring Fun Is Good to the high-starched corporate culture of Major League Baseball, then the philosophy can work anywhere.

Whenever I grow frustrated with the baseball establishment, I take a walk in the outfield and speak aloud to Dad, asking for advice. He used to call me "McGill" after Connie Mack (né Cornelius McGillicuddy), the great Baseball Hall of Fame manager and team owner.

In my mind, I still can hear Dad saying, "You know, McGill . . ."

Some find my conversations with Dad endearing or eccentric. Others believe it's a sign that I've gone mad.

I tell them not to worry. At least not until Dad starts speaking back.

Fun Is Good is organized in three sections. In Part I ("It's All in Your Heart and Head"), we show how to lay the foundation for Fun Is Good in your career and workplace. Whether you're running the show or a cog in the wheel, you'll discover how to find your passions, change your attitude, and think of others in order to make work fun.

In Part II ("Lighten Up"), you'll learn specific ways for your career and business to benefit from Fun Is Good. We'll examine how my dad, Bill Veeck, employed this philosophy in his daily routines and see how this mindset is something that can improve not just your workplace and career but also every aspect of your life. You'll learn how the power of irreverence can help shape careers and businesses.

In Part III ("Spread the Word"), we discuss how to integrate Fun Is Good into your life and how you can spread it throughout your family and workplace.

Part I
. . . .

Fun Is Good:
It's All in Your Heart and Head

FUN IS GOOD isn't just a concept. It's an experience, a feeling, a way of life, and an attitude. When employees of our minor league baseball teams come to work each morning, they know they're going to have fun, whether there's a game that night or not. Without that positive attitude ingrained throughout the organization, their work experience wouldn't be nearly as interesting or productive.

Every organization can implement the Fun Is Good philosophy. Fun Is Good means laughing, joking, keeping things light, and having a positive attitude. But it goes much deeper. It's building relationships and creating an office community. It's treating coworkers and customers the way they should be treated: with dignity and respect. It's taking a proactive, hustling approach to building a career based on your own interests.

In these first four chapters, we show how to create the Fun Is Good atmosphere in your career and workplace.

Chapter 1

What Is Your Passion?

Where do your passions lie? What brings you joy? Consider for a moment where you are at this stage of your life. If during your childhood years you had received a visit from the Ghost of Christmas Future and were able to see where you are right now, how would you have felt?

I bet you might have been at least a little disappointed. (I know I was for a long time.) You probably would not have liked the idea of toiling through your workdays the way you are now. Maybe you ended up exactly where you'd hoped, only to have it not live up to expectations. Either way, you're now wondering where the joy in your life went, at least professionally.

If you're at a point in your career where you're able and willing to make a drastic change, consider using Fun Is Good as your starting point. What would bring you professional happiness? Could you parlay a hobby or leisure interest into a career?

Most of us take the wrong approach to our career. We look at what's out there, and then try to fit ourselves to a role. Shouldn't it be the other way around? We ought to examine what brings us joy, and then find the role where we can best put those passions to work.

I understand that some people have financial responsibilities that make a midlife career change difficult. For you, we'll talk at length about how you can introduce Fun Is Good to any workplace, no matter how seemingly miserable.

Passion is the motivation that drives us to be creative, productive, and efficient at work. Passion keeps us going and helps us accomplish goals and overcome the most difficult challenges.

You might find this hard to believe, but it's possible to combine passion with everyday work. We should all be striving to do that. When we're able to incorporate passion into our work, the benefits are immense. Admittedly, it can be challenging. When faced with a lot of responsibilities and not much time, we can lose focus. By concentrating on more menial tasks, we lose energy, enthusiasm, and sight of the overall vision.

Passion does *not* mean being a workaholic or forcing yourself to enjoy some of the tedious elements of your responsibilities. But with passion, we are better able to understand the big picture and the purpose of these everyday tasks. Having passion enables us to enjoy our work in alignment with our values.

If you're someone still trying to find your way, let your passions serve as your guide. Look for environments where people are having fun. When I hire people, I seek out passionate folks with an array of interests, no matter how eclectic. If I need an accountant, for instance, I don't look for just someone with the proper credentials. I go in search of an experienced accountant with other interests, someone I know might not only be fun to be around but perhaps have nonaccounting skills that might be valuable. Perhaps this person is a fly-fisherman or guitar player. That kind of focus and creativity manifests itself in the workplace.

We've forgotten how important people are. Businesses tend to think it's the product or the technology that's most important, but it's really the people.

It's always the people.

When I conduct interviews, I look for passion, and I can tell within 2 minutes if a person has it. Résumés mean little in our organization. Someone with the most impressive background won't fit if he or she doesn't have passion. At the same time, someone with a modest résumé might be a perfect fit.

I run minor league baseball teams. We're not especially significant in society or even in the world of sports. As an employer, I offer long hours and modest pay, yet I have the pick of the litter when it comes to hiring people.

The reason is that I can offer a precious commodity rarely found in business: laughter. People want to work for us. If you can't make your organization fun, you're going to struggle to attract and retain quality employees unless you can offer large salaries and extensive benefits (and those pale in time). People love working in a relaxed environment and having a job that leaves them smiling.

I was disappointed to see the Internet bubble burst because it was a time people seemed to be having fun in the workplace. Maybe most of them were chasing unrealistic dreams, but that's okay. They had a vision and pursued it with passion. It was a time when ideas were valued, and even though people worked ridiculously long hours, they were having a great time.

When the boom ended, the traditional brick-and-mortar executives smirked at the dressed-down Internet wannabes with the casual offices and Ping-Pong tables in the conference rooms. Yep, the market proved that it was no way to run a business.

Actually, the downturn merely proved that they needed sounder business plans and that the market for Internet commerce wasn't as strong as had once been thought. There was nothing wrong with the Fun Is Good attitude.

I admire the people who took the risk of joining Internet companies. Sure, maybe some of them got what they deserved by hungrily following stock options, but most of them wanted just to be part of something special.

We hear from these people all the time. They're immensely talented but feel disenfranchised from the corporate world. These are the people who will lead you to the money.

Most middle managers hire people who are not as smart or experienced as they are. After all, they don't want anyone to take their jobs.

We take the opposite approach. We hire people who ultimately can take our jobs, who have the smarts and the passion but just need the experience. I've always been fascinated by the Kennedy White House. Even if you're not a fan of JFK, you have to concede that he was a master of assembling talent. He wasn't afraid to hire people intellectually and artistically more gifted. As a result, he ended up with a cabinet that was a combination of these great talents. It was a group of supremely passionate people that contributed to this perception of the White House as Camelot.

Most of us allow life to beat us up and then down. We fall into routines, especially at work, and over time we sleepwalk through much of our lives, especially at work. It's time to shake ourselves out of this mediocre existence.

Let's begin with a trip down memory lane. When you were growing up, what made you happy? What did you gravitate toward in school? Identify strands from your life that brought you happiness. What were your dreams?

Life takes dozens of twists and turns. The one constant is your passion—at least it should be. I start every job interview with the same question: "Do you love baseball?" I run minor league baseball teams, and it stands to reason that if someone wants to work for me, it's probably because they love baseball.

Sometimes someone replies, "Yeah, I like baseball. But I really love football."

That's fine. I'm fortunate to have contacts in the NFL and at various colleges, and if this seems like a passionate person, I'll direct him or her toward the appropriate person because chances are they're going to be more effective and happy working in football than with one of our baseball teams.

The same is true in any field. If you run a flower shop, it seems logical that the people you hire should feel strongly about flowers. They should be passionate about creating arrangements that will produce strong emotional responses from the recipients. They should feel those responses as they construct the arrangement.

Maybe you're in a career that you're not especially passionate about, but you enjoy certain elements of it and want to remain in it for those reasons. Make a list of the 10 things you like about your job. Maybe you're a numbers geek, someone who really enjoys statistics. We have an accountant in our organization who, believe it or not, loves dealing with audits. He lives for battling the IRS and, not surprisingly, is very good at it.

Another accountant might not find the work so fascinating, but maybe that accountant has a passion for sailing. She loves plotting courses and collects old treasure maps. She ought to be helping the company and its clients plot growth, making 3-year and 5-year projections. If that's not enough, maybe she could open up a freelance accounting business that allowed her more time to pursue sailing. Perhaps she could live on a sailboat docked near some of her major clients.

If you can't come up with even a few things you like about your career, then it's time to find something else. It's probably impossible to match your passion with your career, and that's okay. Career change is good, and the sooner you make the commitment to change, the better.

In fact, if fun is good, change is better. We must always keep evolving.

I frequently hear from attorneys who want to work in our organization. They're burned out from working in the legal profession. Maybe they went in with altruistic visions of helping the little guy. Maybe they were mesmerized by Gregory Peck's performance as Atticus Finch in *To Kill a Mockingbird* or attracted by the glamorous portrayal of the legal profession in television shows such as *L. A. Law, Ally McBeal,* and *The Practice.* Maybe they just wanted a decent, well-paying job.

What they come to realize is that they have to work like animals for 8 years to become a partner, and that means they're going to spend 80 hours a week on the job and have no time for their families.

They arrive at age 32 or 35 and get the partnership, yet there's this huge void. They're competitive beyond belief, which isn't necessarily a bad thing, but they have problems with personal relationships and have forgotten how to have fun because they define their lives in terms of billable hours and stamina and haven't engaged in what could be defined as a leisure activity in nearly a decade.

Even professionally, the work isn't fulfilling. They start out with this wide-eyed hope that they're going to make a difference, perhaps engaging in some Hollywood courtroom theatrics, but soon realize most of what they do is just paperwork. Any Fun Is Good elements seen on law-themed TV programs don't exist in real life.

When the lawyers reach their mid-30s, that's when they start looking to escape. It's not just lawyers; it's anyone who has toiled tirelessly to climb the corporate ladder. They get to the point where the money no longer matters. They're willing to trade that six-figure salary to work for $25,000 in minor league baseball or wherever their true passions lie.

Believe me, I know what it's like not to have that career satisfaction. I spent a decade in advertising and worked to the point where in 1989, at the age of 38, I earned $90,000. But I wasn't happy, and when I got the opportunity to run a minor league baseball team for $25,000, I grabbed it and never looked back.

If you're just getting out of high school or college, there's no better time to pursue a career based on your passions. You're so much more technically savvy and immersed in media than previous generations that you have a much better idea of what's out there and what you want.

Maybe you've seen one of your parents unceremoniously released from a job after many years of service. Maybe you've seen one of them lose a pension or 401(k) because the company squandered it or did something unethical that resulted in the stock's becoming worthless.

There are people who have lost millions in retirement funds because of corporate mismanagement, and suddenly they have to rebuild their lives. At least if they had a good time amassing that fortune, they'll have the energy to do it again. If they hated it and were counting the days to retirement, they're left bitter and feeling hopeless.

It's never too late. Colonel Harland Sanders did not begin actively franchising the business that became Kentucky Fried Chicken (and later KFC) until the age of 65.

There comes a time in everyone's life where you must take a hard look at where you've been and where you're going. We have a lot better recall of our emotions than facts. We know when we were happy and when we were depressed. There were times when we were carefree and childlike and willing to take chances.

If you're unhappy, you might think you can't afford to take that chance. In reality, you can't afford to stay where you are. Even if it means you'll take a short-term hit financially or move to another part of the country, the upside in terms of your happiness will be worth it tenfold.

We see this all the time in our organization—one that offers long hours, hard work, and modest pay, but also a Fun Is Good atmosphere that unleashes passions. Many people who have worked for our organization have gone on to successful careers in every industry imaginable. (This isn't because they didn't like working for us, but because they saw a way to apply our formula to other businesses. In fact, our average tenure is much longer than in a typical workplace.) Others came to us after struggling to find professional fulfillment elsewhere. The common denominator is they never gave up on the dream of finding a career and a workplace where they could have fun.

When most people enter the job market, they rarely use passion as a guide. They follow in the footsteps of a family member or pursue a career because of its financial upside or perceived value in society.

As college students, they fill out those vaguely worded standardized tests that are supposed to match personality traits with jobs. Inevitably, they're told that their skills and personality traits make them best qualified to become, say, an astronaut or funeral director.

College kids also spend a lot of time trying to impress on-campus recruiters, as if such visitors represent the only employment opportunities out there. They try to say the right things and convince these potential employers that, yes indeed, they've always longed to work in (whatever field or industry) and have a burning desire to do so.

It's tough to fake passion. Maybe you can put on an act long enough to get the job, but it's impossible to maintain it. Instead of trying to match someone else's demands, why not try and find something that fits your passions?

If you approach your career that way, whether you're just starting out or making a change, you'll have a greater chance at becoming successful. The early pioneers in computers and technology did not set out to become wealthy. They were the guys who had a passion for taking apart radios in their garages.

My friend Dave Dombrowski, whom you'll hear from later in this book, did not set out to become a highly paid sports executive. But he did identify a passion for sports at the age of 6 and knew he wanted to become a general manager of a Major League Baseball team, even though such work was not especially high paying when Dave set that goal.

Passion is the cornerstone of the Fun Is Good philosophy, and if you let it be your guide, you'll achieve success. Throughout this book, we'll hear firsthand from people like Dave who have benefited professionally and personally from the Fun Is Good philosophy and how they applied it specifically to their industries and careers.

. . . .

FUN IS GOOD VIGNETTE

Tom Whaley,
Vice President, St. Paul Saints

"The thing I love about the Fun Is Good philosophy is that it embraces misfits like me."

In the early 1990s, I had my own private law practice in Minnesota and was miserable. Like a lot of young attorneys, I went into the law profession thinking that I could make a difference—that I could somehow change things for the better.

In reality, being a lawyer is rarely about change; it's mostly mind-numbing briefs and arguments with disagreeable personalities. When my dad, a successful lawyer, had a debilitating stroke at age 51, I knew I had to do what I loved. He'd always say, "Have fun; you could get hit by a bus today." I've been running from the bus ever since.

People find it hard to believe that I'm a lawyer, and I take that as a compliment. I'm more comfortable in jeans, T-shirts, and 3-day-old stubble. I play drums in a rock band, and I'd much rather argue about whether Rush belongs in the Rock 'n' Roll Hall of Fame than the Rule against Perpetuities.

I knew I didn't fit in as a lawyer, at least not in the traditional sense. I had heard about Mike Veeck and the Northern League, and I figured there must be a place for me in his zany organization. When it was announced shortly before the Christmas holidays that the Goldklang Group would own the new St. Paul Saints in 1993, I wrote Mike a letter.

I knew I had just one chance to make an impression, so I bought some frozen lutefisk, this nasty-tasting Scandinavian dish that consists of dried cod soaked in lye. I included a copy of my résumé with a note that said, "This is what people in Minnesota eat," wrapped it in dry ice, and sent it to Florida, where Mike was still working.

Mike called the next afternoon from Pott's Place, a saloon near the ballpark; he was in the process of being moved by the holiday spirit.

"Tom, what is this?"

"It's fish, Mike, seafood."

"Tom, I live in Florida and know a thing or two about seafood and this is not seafood. It's thawing on the bar. We're paying people 5 bucks if they have a taste. There's a guy over in the corner who tried it. He's either very drunk or dead."

A few days later, I received a letter.

"I hate attorneys," he wrote, "but you seem like a Renaissance lawyer, which intrigues me. We've got this thing going in the Northern League, so call me and I can show you how to ruin your life."

Even though I had a wife and two young kids, I quit my law practice, took a massive pay cut, and joined the circus. Our first office consisted of two phones and a few folding chairs.

In my new role, I still practiced law; like everyone else in minor league baseball, I also did a little bit of everything. At one point during our first season, I had to find a St. Bernard between the hours of midnight and 6 a.m. that Bill Murray could use in an on-field skit. I learned to move fast, have little fear, and get things done.

I learned from Mike how to promote concerts, a key side business in minor league baseball. Along the way, we started running a massive three-on-three basketball tournament.

In 1999, I followed Mike to Florida when he joined the Tampa Bay Devil Rays. When Mike resigned after a short but controversial tenure, I didn't know what to do. Since I was viewed as one of "Mike's guys"—

and made little secret of the fact—I figured it made no sense for me to stay.

Before I could clean out my desk, the phone rang. It was Bill Murray, who was trying to find out what had happened to Mike. I explained my predicament.

"Stay put for another year if you can," he said.

I was incredulous. "Are you kidding me?"

Murray explained that he had probably stayed one year too long at Saturday Night Live. His best friends had left, people were making mistakes, and he wasn't having nearly as much fun. But in that year, he said he learned more about the television business than at any other point in his career.

"Stick around and pay attention to how things are done, even if they're being done the wrong way," he said. "You'll learn what not to do, which usually is more important."

When Bill Murray is offering you career advice based on his tenure during the golden age of SNL, you know your life is on the right track.

Bill was right, of course. I hung around for another year, learned a lot—good and bad—then returned to St. Paul and rejoined the circus. These days, I'm a part owner of several of our minor league baseball teams.

Would I be a wealthier man if I had kept my law business? Probably, though it wouldn't be nearly as much fun. The stress and the pressure would have gotten to me. I haven't been to work in 13 years—at least it doesn't seem like work. I go to my office at the ballpark and have fun.

I hear so many people say "if only." If only they could quit their jobs and do something else, they'd be happy. It's not easy to walk away. But the thing that clinched it for me was realizing that I might be the one who has the stroke. There is no tomorrow, and if you wait around to chase your dream, it's just not going to happen.

● ●

Like Tom Whaley (see the "Fun Is Good Vignette" above), you need to take a proactive approach to applying your passion to your career. Fun Is Good is not just for people who own or operate businesses. It's more applicable to those who work for them.

Search for those organizations where you can not only apply your talents but also have fun. They don't have to be mutually exclusive. Tom took a risk by leaving the certainty and security of a traditional law practice, but he knew if he could find somewhere to best apply his passions and skills—all of his skills—he'd be happier and better off in the long run.

People shortchange themselves when it comes to marketing their skills and choosing a career. They think, "I have a degree in accounting; therefore I am an accountant or some sort of finance person." They forget about their other skills, talents, and experiences, things that on the surface might seem to have nothing to do with their work.

Tom plays in rock-and-roll bands. He has a passion for music. These days, he organizes and promotes concerts in all of our ballparks. His people skills are so good that he can perform (and has) most every role in our organization. He's still a lawyer, but the difference is that he's involved with legal work he thoroughly enjoys.

I know it's difficult, perhaps impossible in some cases, to leave a job. If that's the case, think of how you can revamp your current situation. Do your colleagues and managers know about other skills and experiences you have that might make you more valuable in another role, one you might enjoy more? Could you prove your worth in a different area by latching on to a different project, even if it's in addition to your current work?

Fun Is Good can work anywhere and for anyone. Regardless of whether the owners and managers subscribe to the philosophy, it's still up to the employees to take a proactive approach to injecting this concept into their careers and finding a way to pursue their passion within a career.

Throughout this book, we'll show how that's possible.

. . . .

Fun Is Good Interview

If you want to create Fun Is Good at your company or go to work at a place where such an attitude exists, then it's time to overhaul the job interview process.

If you're the employer, get rid of the stilted, ambiguous questions about strengths and weaknesses. Instead ask candidates about the last book they read or movie they saw. Ask them what they do on a Saturday afternoon. Get them talking about their passions. This is how you find well-rounded, eclectic people that can help your business far beyond what's listed in the job description.

When sports teams draft kids out of high school or college, they talk about drafting for a specific need or position or just taking "the best player available." Companies should look for the best person available. If you're searching for an accountant and take a tunnel-vision approach to finding one, then that's what you're going to get. But if you find a Renaissance person who just happens to have accounting skills, you end up with a person who can help in many other areas and perhaps become a star.

If you're the prospective employee, turn the interview process on its head. You should be the one asking the questions. Too often the person wants the job—any job—so badly they take whatever is available, regardless of how unappetizing.

To find that Fun Is Good environment, you need to be selective and thorough in the job search process. Think of it as you interviewing prospective employers, not vice versa.

What does the office do as a group for fun? Are there any company-wide volunteering projects? Are there any people here with unconventional backgrounds? How does it celebrate success? Is mentoring common? Are they visible in the community? Are there women in positions of power?

The answers to those questions reveal how much of the "we're all in this together" attitude exists and the value, if any, the company places on community service. It speaks volumes if the employer knows little about their colleagues' outside interests.

Ask if the company has teams in sports leagues. Does it have a health club? You want to see what value the business places on teamwork, employee health, and social get-togethers.

Ask about meetings. How many are there? Are they all-inclusive? You don't want to join a place that's bogged down with meetings. At the same time, you want to know what value they place on ideas, no matter who presents them.

Don't ask about the annual review process; it makes you look like you're counting the days to your first raise. When the interviewer asks where you want to be in 3 or 5 years, turn the question around. Ask if employees typically develop mentoring relationships with those who can help them plot their course.

In our organization, we encourage people to draw up personal marketing plans and review them periodically with me. This might not always be possible with larger organizations, but it should be done at some level.

How do ideas flow? If you have a great idea for a promotion or to improve a part of the company, how should you present it? Does the company have contests for such things?

You can research much of this beforehand. Did the folks at the top start at the bottom? You want to know if the company hires from outside or nurtures its own.

Look around the office. How is it decorated? Do people have their kids' artwork posted? This not only speaks volumes about the emphasis on family but also shows that the people don't take themselves too seriously.

Ask to speak to people in different departments, especially customer service. Note the value given to this area. A company that ignores customer service won't be around for the long haul.

Schedule your interview around lunchtime or during off hours. Who is still around? Are they having fun? How much laughter do you hear while you're there?

Above all else, take an interest in the people you meet. Ask them about their hobbies and family. If you're in the same business, chances are you have mutual acquaintances. Look around their offices for topics of conversation, especially shared interests. Show that you're someone who takes a sincere interest in others.

Remember, the goal is for you to get to know these people better, not to talk about yourself. If you're inquisitive and show a genuine interest in people, not just the company, you'll make a positive first impression.

More important, you'll gather all the information you need to determine if this is a Fun Is Good place or not.

· ·

FUN IS GOOD

Chapter 1 Summary and Exercises (What Is Your Passion?)

- Outside of family, name five things you're passionate about.
- Do those passions relate to your career?
- What would you like to do professionally? Are you doing it now?
- Can you turn a hobby into a career? How?
- If not, can the expertise and passion from that hobby be applied to your job? (Think of the sailing accountant.)
- Think back to the times in your life that you were happiest professionally. What about your career made you happy?
- What about your current job excites you? Does it make you more productive?
- If you enjoy nothing about your job, what would you like to do?
- When you go into a job interview, turn the process upside down and do most of the questioning yourself.
- If you're an employer, look for well-rounded people, not just the best fit for the position.

Chapter 2

The Right Attitude

When it comes to implementing Fun Is Good in your workplace and career, attitude is everything.

Having a positive attitude is the foundation for successful relationships with your organization and coworkers. How your day unfolds depends on your attitude. When people come to work complaining, avoiding coworkers, and making it apparent they can't wait to get home, it hurts them and everyone around them.

Attitude is contagious, whether positive or negative. One negative attitude can dampen the enthusiasm of an entire office. When someone comes to work with a negative attitude, it's that person's responsibility to recognize it and turn it around.

A negative attitude affects every aspect of life and work. At work, it decreases your potential for success. A bad attitude contributes to unhappiness at the office, which is inevitably brought home, where it impacts the family.

Attitude has a huge impact on business. It's much more enjoyable to deal with upbeat, genuinely positive people—not those who half-heartedly say "have a nice day" at the end of a transaction or wear those insufferable smiley-face buttons that make me want to jab a dagger through them. Who wants to do business with someone with a bad attitude?

A positive attitude has a tremendous impact. Admittedly, it's not always easy to remain upbeat. There are ups and downs in all aspects of life, but a positive outlook makes getting through the tough times easier. Not only that, but it helps build rapport with clients and coworkers and brings about a clear, healthy mindset that generates and unleashes creativity.

In our organization, we believe that "Attitude is 90 percent of life." Talent and perseverance play a role, to be sure, but talent means little if you don't have the right attitude. Every office has a couple of people who are supremely talented but never get anywhere because of their attitudes.

Part of having a good attitude means understanding the difference between taking your responsibilities seriously and taking yourself too seriously. With that mentality, it's easier to laugh and deal with obstacles.

Think of someone you know who is constantly upbeat. What you'll find is someone who is genuinely interested in the world and other people. They're comfortable in their own skins. They lighten up a workplace and make it more enjoyable. This happens in sports all the time, where a gregarious new player helps loosen up a tight, stressful locker room.

When I worked for the Chicago White Sox in 1977, we acquired a player named Oscar Gamble. Oscar was an outgoing, fun-loving guy who made life more enjoyable for everyone around him. Between his personality and huge Afro, which looked rather funny bulging out from under the sides of his baseball hat, Oscar turned out to be just the type of memorable person you'd expect from someone with a cool name like Oscar Gamble.

The Oscar Gambles are the opposite of those who are constantly creating chaos and trouble around them to make others as miserable as they are.

I used to be one of those people: I wanted the world around me in turmoil because that's how it was for me. Now I want to be as far from turmoil as I can be. I want things to be peaceful and happy because that's the environment that makes me most creative.

It takes effort to wake up and be in a lousy mood. After all, it requires more muscles to frown than it does to smile. Granted, it takes some work to become one of those upbeat people. Like anything else, the process becomes easier if you find a role model.

During the 6 years I spent working for my father with the Chicago White Sox, I never once saw him in a lousy mood. If you can emulate a person like that, pretty soon that's the cloak you will wear. People have a driving need to be happy, and it's a tough act to pull off if it's not genuine.

So how do you pull it off? First, find that role model. Second, try and hang out with people who are more upbeat than you. Third, try to find something to laugh about or have fun with in everything you do.

Even in times of stress, it's possible to take a moment and enjoy something about it. If you're involved in a fender-bender, there's nothing about it that's going to make you happy. You're late for work. The car is a mess. The other person doesn't have car insurance. It's tough to find something positive there.

Let's say you're trying to get out the door in the morning and can't find the car keys. As a result, you miss the first train into town. Instead of stressing about it, why not take the opposite approach and laugh at yourself? View it as though you're destined to have a little adventure today.

During the writing of this book, my coauthor and his family spent a week with my family and me. One morning, his toddler was up early and crying. I was lying in bed one floor below, and I suppose if I had let it bother me, I could have been upset that the little guy was keeping me awake. Instead, it brought back a flood of memories of when my daughter was that age.

Why not take every moment and enjoy something about it? People make the mistake of viewing life as just a series of goals. If I just get this promotion or house or job, I'm going to be happy. Life doesn't work that way. It's the journey that matters, and how you approach it makes all the difference. The big house, look-at-me car—those things are never enough.

Instead of brooding over something negative, it's much easier to say, "I think I'll have some fun with this."

Years ago, Sammy Davis Jr. performed in St. Paul, Minnesota, right after a blizzard. More than 5,000 tickets had been sold, but only 300 people showed up because of the road conditions. People in St. Paul are conditioned to drive in anything, but this was so bad most of them stayed home.

Sammy could have called off the show, done an abbreviated version, or simply gone through the motions. Instead, he walked on stage and announced, "Thank you so much for coming. I know it wasn't easy, so I'm going to put on a show you won't believe so that you can tell everyone what they missed."

He performed for nearly 3 hours and was spectacular.

Attitude is everything. One of the great lessons in life is that as you get older, time seems to pass more quickly. The key is to approach life as the great adventure that it is. Recognize that if you go to a job that you love, the trip becomes the reward.

At the end of my 35 years in baseball, I'm not going to look back and admire my nice house or wish I had bought that Jaguar convertible. I'm going to look back at all the people I shared a few laughs with, all of the kids I (hopefully) inspired and those who inspired me. The material rewards obtained and goals not reached won't matter.

Everyone has a few elements of their jobs that make them uncomfortable. It's tough to approach them with a good attitude and a sense of humor.

In my business, it's releasing players. Some of these guys are a joy to be around, grasp the Fun Is Good mentality, and are willing to do anything to make the fans' experience memorable. Unfortunately, if they're not performing on the field, it doesn't matter. Baseball has a cruel but efficient way of weeding people out that way. The numbers don't lie.

Maybe you have to fire people. Perhaps some of those people have good attitudes, but the business or economy has changed and they no longer fit.

It's painful telling people that they're no longer wanted and need to find another line of work, or at least another employer. The process is difficult, but if you bring a positive attitude to the situation, it becomes easier.

I let the person dictate the terms of departure, and that makes an uncomfortable situation go more smoothly. Usually people you're releasing are on the bubble—they're ready to go and often are relieved to get the news. If you've been at a job 2 or 3 years and the passion no longer is there or never caught on to begin with, then being fired actually is a favor.

Dad was a master at this. In 1978, the White Sox were not playing well and Dad summoned his good friend, manager Bob

Lemon, to a meeting. After a few hours of cheerful conversation that involved more than a few adult beverages, Lemon smiled.

"It's been fun, Bill."

Lemon knew why he was there. A few weeks later, George Steinbrenner hired Lemon to manage the New York Yankees. A few months after that, Lemon guided the Bronx Bombers to a World Series championship.

Talk about landing on your feet.

There was nothing wrong with Bob Lemon's attitude, but negative attitudes in the workplace are contagious, and that's especially a problem if you've developed a reputation for running a Fun Is Good company where everyone is making an effort to maintain upbeat attitudes.

Maybe you have this negative person, perhaps with lots of talent, so you try to give him the benefit of the doubt. The best thing to do is to cut him out instantly. Let him know that he's affecting the way the business is running.

If not, you run the risk of throwing off the delicate balance that is a harmonious office. If you keep this person around, it's going to breed resentment from the folks who are having fun at work and fostering the environment that is so vital for personal and professional fulfillment.

Your attitude permeates every element of your being and extends to every aspect of life. Here's one way to improve it quickly:

Imagine a glass bowl, preferably a round aquarium that might hold a goldfish or two, filled with marbles. Each marble should represent a remaining week of your life. For the sake of this exercise, we'll assume we're going to live for 70 years. So, if you're 50, put 1,040 marbles in the bowl. At the end of each week, remove a marble.

People have used variations of this exercise to illustrate how life is slipping away, faster than we realize it. The marble bowl is a tough image to shake because you see how much time you have left—at least according to the average life expectancy. Once you've visualized the end, you realize how important it is not to waste time.

You develop a sense of urgency, not to the point where you're anxious and concerned about the sand slipping through the hourglass. Instead, you become more productive and bring the proper attitude and perspective to your work.

"Losing your marbles" usually refers to a loss of sanity or coherent thought, which happens all too often in the corporate world.

There was a great movie a few years back called *Office Space* that did a spot-on job of channeling the frustrations of office workers. Some were in their mid-20s and already beaten down by the bureaucracy and repetition of their jobs. There was a middle manager in his 40s who could not explain to a couple of outside consultants what exactly he did. There were layers upon layers of managers that turned a once-productive office, in this case a technology company, into one endless series of memos and paperwork.

The frustrations simmered until a group of young employees installed a virus in the company mainframe and funneled hundreds of thousands of dollars into their personal accounts. The middle manager without a job description contemplated suicide, only to become an instant millionaire in a settlement from an automobile accident. Another long-ignored employee finally had enough and burned the office down.

Office Space was a darkly humorous film because it made fun of the frustrations common to so many workplaces. Peter Gibbons, the lead character played by Ron Livingston, summed it up perfectly: "Human beings weren't meant to sit in little cubicles, staring at computer screens all day, filling out useless forms and listening to eight different bosses drone on about mission statements."

Everyone can relate to that. I worked in Major League Baseball, which has taken corporate bureaucracy to the level of an art form.

The characters in *Office Space* dealt with the frustrations in self-destructive, illegal ways. That's a natural reaction when you look at yourself as the victim. Whining about your job has become a natural pastime. Why not do something about it?

Think of the level of the marbles in the bowl going down.

Once you give up control of your career to someone else, it becomes a mindset. You're defeated already, at the mercy of the corporate welfare state.

If you decide at 30 or 40 or 50 that you've had enough and are not going to take it anymore, that's a great start. You're regaining control. If you start a business and do something you've always wanted to do, you're suddenly wiser and should start making plans for 5 and 10 years down the road. Write down goals—things you expect and want to happen.

Now you're not just casting your fate to the wind and genetics; you're in control of it. Most of us are fairly responsible when it comes to planning. We write wills, start college funds for our children, and contribute to retirement accounts.

Yet when it comes to careers, there's little long-term planning. Everybody knows exactly where they want to be at 65, but not 45 or 55. Nobody thinks about those stages because they're resigned to sleepwalking through an *Office Space* existence for a few decades.

That's a dangerous mindset, especially now that you can't rely on a lengthy corporate existence followed by a pension and cushy retirement.

Lots of people dream of being entrepreneurial, but few take the leap. Taking the first step is the hard part. The rest is easy because things move so fast you don't have time to think about whether it will succeed or fail. The only scary step is the first one, when you jump off the high board. The moment you let go, there's something exhilarating and refreshing.

People refuse to make that leap because they're trained to believe that the rate of failure is high, which it is, and that it's a terrible thing.

So what? Think of the most successful deceased person. The world continues to go on, without missing a beat, and there's something reassuring about the continuity of that process.

So don't sit by and be an observer. If you don't make the most of your skills, some employer is going to use them and not provide you with the wherewithal to take care of yourself.

That inspires many people to take the entrepreneurial plunge. If that seems too daunting, try to get a piece of the action where you are. Is it possible for you to have an ownership stake? Stand up and tell the boss that you deserve to be a partner in this endeavor (assuming that you do). You don't have to come across as arrogant or demanding; just calmly point out that your contributions to the company are important and that you'd like to share more in the rewards, perhaps as a limited partner.

Assuming, of course, that you don't work for a large, publicly held company, you'll be either invited to reap the rewards or turned down. If rejection is the answer, you'll have the extra push to be entrepreneurial. Either way, you'll be better off.

A neighbor of mine recently put this philosophy to work. I did not know the gentleman that well, but he came to visit me in the hospital after I had suffered a serious leg injury. He was employed by a large insurance business and had grown frustrated that his work was not appreciated.

Though I was heavily medicated and don't remember much of the conversation, I apparently asked him if he had a handful of clients that would go with him if he started his own business or joined a company that would give him an ownership stake.

He nodded and apparently moved quickly to make a change because a few days later he flagged down my wife, Libby, in her car and told her about how he had taken my advice and now had an ownership interest at his new employer.

Thankfully, things worked out. It's a good thing I didn't recommend anything more drastic while in a painkiller-induced haze.

The episode is another example of how we're losing our marbles, sometimes in more ways than one. Since we have only so much time, why not lose our marbles on our own terms?

. . . .

Boosting Attitude—
and Customer Service along the Way

A few years ago, Delta Airlines sent its frequent flyers books of postcards. Each time the travelers received excellent customer service or encountered Delta employees with great attitudes going beyond the call of duty, they handed that employee a postcard.

Presumably, the employees who obtained the greatest number of postcards received prizes. I'm not sure what Delta awarded, but I know a similar promotion worked wonders in our organization.

Jim Lucas, who was the assistant general manager of our Charleston RiverDogs team a few years ago, issued pins to 10 or 15 fans before each game, with instructions to give them to employees who provided great customer service. The 3 employees who collected the most pins at the end of the season received cash prizes.

These pins cost us only about 60 cents apiece, but you would have thought they were precious gemstones. Employees proudly displayed them on hats and worked tirelessly to obtain them. Since nobody knew who had the pins, everyone was treated extraordinarily well by employees with upbeat attitudes.

Granted, our organization prides itself on customer service, but the pins took things to another level. Soon we introduced the pins at all of our ballparks. Fans marveled at how everyone seemed to know their names and worked so hard to make their experiences at the ballpark memorable.

Any company can incorporate such a promotion. It's remarkable how it can improve attitudes in the workplace.

When Lucas moved to our ball club in Brockton, Massachusetts, he decided everyone would take 90 minutes for lunch. His reasoning was that most people wanted to have time for lunch and to exercise. Most didn't have time to work out in the morning because they were getting kids off to school. By the time they got home, they were too exhausted.

We work people beyond their limits in our business, especially during the baseball season. By providing this extra 30 minutes, we gave them the opportunity to stay in shape, work off stress, and get away from the office. It wasn't just altruistic; healthy employees are more productive.

My coauthor, Pete Williams, used to work at USA Today, where they provide employees with a cutting edge health club for the princely sum of about $15 a month. The fee even included laundry service. There was no excuse not to work out.

It's tough to have a bad attitude when you've just knocked yourself out on the treadmill or by lifting weights for an hour. The endorphin rush doesn't allow it.

I can hear Corporate America shuddering at this idea. "Ninety minutes for lunch! People will take advantage of the situation." I disagree. You restrict people to 45 minutes for lunch, and you'll be the one who has disgruntled employees who steal stamps and office supplies.

If employees have incentives to bolster their attitudes, the company will be repaid tenfold.

· ·

Fun Is Good Vignette

Pete Orme,
Charter Sales Manager, Grand Excursion

"During my 5-year stint with the St. Paul Saints, I occasionally was called upon to scrape bird droppings off seats. After rain delays, I would head to the outfield with brooms, squeegees, and a couple of colleagues, and stand ankle-deep in water as we tried to prepare the field for play."

Inevitably, one of us would gaze skyward and think of one of the many young adults who marveled at how cool our jobs were.

"So you still want to work in sports?" one of us would ask.

"Fun Is Good," someone would reply.

When you enjoy your job, even the worst aspects of it don't seem that bad. And if you can maintain that Fun Is Good attitude, it gets you through the tough spots.

I work for Grand Excursion, a week-long celebration that marks the 150th anniversary of the 1854 steamboat expedition that brought worldwide attention to what was then America's wild, western frontier. It's not always as fun as working in baseball, but the Fun Is Good philosophy still applies, whether it's in marketing and promotion or simply in our office environment.

To promote the event, we've trumpeted the once-in-a-life-time aspect. "Unless you're 150 years old, you've never been part of something like this," our ads read.

I've found the Fun Is Good attitude to be a powerful tool in keeping morale high and workplace tension from festering into something serious. The key is to not take yourself so seriously. Go all out with your job, but realize that it's okay to have fun doing it.

Years ago, I took one of those standardized tests that are supposed to tell you what career you're best suited for based on personality profiling. I don't remember what career the machine told me I should pursue, but it did a good job pegging me as a peacemaker, a lighthearted guy who can break the ice when things get tense. That's been one of my strengths.

Recently we had some layoffs for budgetary reasons, and some popular people were let go. As expected, this damaged morale and caused the remaining employees to wonder who might be next out the door.

I walked past a group of these people, one of whom said, "Pete, it looks like the ax is swinging."

I winked. "Keep your head low."

It was a subtle gesture, but it earned a few smiles. My point was that you have to remain upbeat and positive. Job security—or lack thereof—is no laughing matter, but irreverence helps. After all, the worst thing that can happen is that you'll lose your job, and few people have ever avoided that experience.

Heck, losing a job can be a positive thing, especially if your current position lacks that fun atmosphere. It can be an opportunity to find that work environment that fits your special talents, goals, strengths, and attitudes. Granted, people are not always going to get along, and things won't always be rosy. But life's too short to stay in a situation where you're not happy.

Throughout the planning for Grand Excursion, I tried to think of what we could do that might be remembered 150 years from now—or at least 10 years down the road. After all, no one is going to remember the office turf battles and other things that seem so important, but they might remember if they laughed and had a good time.

I learned that from Mike Veeck. One night with the Saints, I staged a contest on the field between innings that bombed. It just wasn't funny. People laughed, but it was because it was stupid, not funny.

Later I was apologizing to Mike.

"Were the people laughing?" he asked.

"Yes, but not—"

"Do you think they enjoyed it?"

"Well, yeah," I said.

"Then that's all that matters. Tomorrow they'll think of the great time they had at our game and that they laughed."

He was right. I don't even remember the specifics of the promotion, just the reaction and the power of irreverence. If we can laugh more in the workplace, that's what we'll remember most long after the job is done.

• •

FUN IS GOOD

Chapter 2 Summary and Exercises (The Right Attitude)

- Attitude is 90 percent of life.
- Take your career seriously; *don't* take yourself too seriously.
- Look at life as an hourglass or a bowl of marbles. It brings about a sense of urgency.
- Have you mapped out your career as carefully as you've planned your retirement? If not, where do you want to be at the ages of 30, 40, 50, and 60?
- Recognize that the journey is the reward.
- Find someone with a perpetually upbeat attitude and emulate them.
- Think back to a stressful period. How did laughter or the right attitude help you get through it? Try to find something to laugh at in every situation.
- The next time something disrupts your plans, don't look at it as stress or an intrusion but as a new adventure.
- Instead of brooding over something negative, ask yourself how you can have fun with it.
- Try to exercise every day. It's the single best way to improve your attitude.
- Try to make at least one person laugh every day.

Chapter 3

Chiefs and Indians

N ow that we've addressed our passions and worked on our attitudes, it's time to implement Fun Is Good throughout our business.

Employers have not provided workplaces that are fun. How you make a living is directly connected to your soul, and it's a terrible thing to work in a soulless environment. Everyone reaches a point where the money no longer matters. We want to be happy at all costs.

People often are skeptical about how they can implement Fun Is Good, especially if they're not running the show. It's a lot easier, they suggest, if the first person to buy into Fun Is Good is the chief, not one of the Indians.

That's true in many instances, but it's also possible to lead the charge for change at the lower levels. If that's not possible, then go somewhere else where it might be.

In our organization, we never have titles on our business cards, and it's a wonderful thing because it gives everyone a feeling of equality. Everyone knows who's the boss, right? So why do we feel the need to validate ourselves by coming up with lofty-sounding titles?

We've designed Fun Is Good to be used by both chiefs and Indians. Fun Is Good is not about staging palace coups. It's also not

65

something that necessarily comes about overnight. It's a more subtle process.

It starts with the design of the office. If possible, tear down the dividers; open up the cubicles. The problem with most offices is that everyone is fighting for private space. There's a lot of mistrust because it's assumed people in the private offices are keeping information away from others.

It's better to have as much interaction as possible so people don't feel threatened. Don't put the executives on one floor and everyone else on another. If you absolutely need private space, use a conference room.

If you have a private office, make it inviting. Have space for people to congregate. Put the coffee machine or a candy jar in your office. It forces people to come in and say hello. If small talk does not come easy to you, put the coffeemaker on your desk, and soon people will be coming by to chat.

Place a tray of candy, gum, and mints at the side of your desk. Encourage people to take some or leave contributions. Leave a few toys on your desk. They need not look unprofessional; I know a woman who keeps beach balls printed as globes on her desk.

The idea is not to turn your office into a coffee shop or play area, but to create a harmonious atmosphere in which coworkers feel comfortable interacting. You don't have to be serious all the time. If you can have an irreverent atmosphere, you'll go a long way toward implementing the Fun Is Good mentality in your workplace, no matter how seemingly sterile.

I'd much rather walk into someone's office and see a Nerf basketball hoop on the back of the door and a Bart Simpson doll on the shelf than a bunch of framed diplomas. I'd much prefer to see artwork from a young child posted on the door than a vanity wall of awards and plaques. I'd rather hear music than Muzak.

These signs indicate that Fun Is Good prevails in this office; I know instantly that the person has a sense of humor or is a proud parent, which means he has his priorities straight.

Now you might argue that your business is too serious for all of this. Oh, really? There's a reason pediatricians paint cartoon characters on the wall, wear wacky ties, and keep children's books and toys in their examination rooms: It makes the "customers" feel more at ease. I often wish I had some of those elements in my sterile examination room when I'm sitting there in a flimsy gown feeling a draft up my backside while waiting for the doctor.

There's no reason the office of a lawyer or financial planner can't include a few Fun Is Good touches. How about a gumball machine? It sends a message that even though you take your work seriously, you still have a sense of irreverence.

Not only that, but it's a good icebreaker. There's always that awkward first moment in any initial business contact where you make small talk in order to at least give the impression that you're genuinely interested in the other person—and hopefully you are—and not just there to cut to the chase. Why not give people an opening? It beats talking about the weather.

For instance, I love books. My office looks like a library, and everyone in our organization knows that they can treat it as such. Books come and go. Everyone measures success in their own way; for me it was when I could go to a bookstore and drop $100 on hardback books. Visitors to my office need only look at the titles on my shelf to have an instant conversation topic.

Kids can be another effective icebreaker. A company's approach to children and the policies they have tell you a lot about the people running the show.

My daughter, Rebecca, was not even 2 years old during the summer of 1993, the inaugural season of the St. Paul Saints. She spent many afternoons in a playpen near the entrance to the office. Each time someone entered, she popped up and said "Hi!"

This was not creative marketing genius; we needed to put her somewhere in order to get work done during that first crazy year, and thankfully, there was always a Saints employee somewhere nearby. But the result was that people were left with a favorable, friendly first impression of our organization.

For some reason, we hired a consultant that year to come in and tell us how we could run our business better. He walked in and a little blonde head popped up and said hi.

The first line on the consultant's report was that the kid had to go. We had paid thousands of dollars for this report. The consultant saw Rebecca as totally unprofessional. What he failed to realize was that we were a business where everyone was welcome. Kids were our lifeblood.

Rebecca remained "employed" with the St. Paul Saints. We fired the consultant.

Some companies put a pool table or Ping-Pong table in the office. Those are great stress releases and they build camaraderie, but the most important thing is that it fosters an atmosphere where coworkers take a genuine interest in one another.

It's not enough to just add toys and diversions. There has to be accessibility. In our organization, we try to make as many of our financial and internal documents available to employees as possible. Some might see this as opening a can of worms, but we've actually found many employees aren't interested; it's just more reading material.

When I worked for the Florida Marlins, we actually offered incentives to employees to read them. We would insert a line on page 23 of our latest marketing plan telling readers that the first 11 employees to mention the page receive a free T-shirt.

Any company can do this. Will some employees let the secret out? Perhaps, but there's a chance that they'll really evaluate that marketing plan and give valuable feedback.

You should want feedback. We're not big on meetings in our organization; we believe having fewer meetings is the way to go. The key is to make meetings all-inclusive. A promotions meeting open only to the promotions department is doomed to failure. It offers predictability, not creativity; but if you open it to everyone, you're likely to get more good ideas.

Keep meetings succinct and to the point. Don't have a weekly staff meeting just for the sake of having a weekly staff meeting. Schedule meetings on Friday afternoons. Serve refreshments. Go to a restaurant or take a walk in the park. Do something to break the monotony and make the meetings fun.

Meetings and routine are the enemies of Fun Is Good. So many organizations start out with the Fun Is Good attitude. There's an all-for-one mentality that pervades the organization during those early days, and everyone is excited and working together.

Unfortunately, the hierarchy gradually develops. There are meetings for everything and meetings that don't seem to be about anything. Only certain people are invited to meetings. Employees not included begin to distrust those who are.

The key to any successful Fun Is Good organization is that the Indians have to believe they can become chiefs. We move people around our organization constantly, not just for the sake of keeping people fresh but because it gives them an opportunity to acquire new skills and move up.

People are attracted to our company because they look at it and say, "I can move up with this group." They see high-ranking employees who started as interns, or sales people now running the show. Show me a magazine that's run by a former intern or copy aide, and I'll show you a successful publication.

It's important to blur the line between chief and Indian. The chiefs need to go out and work the front lines so that the Indians know there's not a single job out there that the chief hasn't done. The chiefs *should* be dealing with customers.

I'll often go out before our games and take tickets, not because I'm recognized or because I'm a shameless self-promoter looking for a photo opportunity, but because it's a way for me to pitch in and to get feedback on our organization from fans. It's also fun.

Do employees know that I'm the boss, and is there a little bit of fear that comes from that relationship? Absolutely. But they also know that I won't ask them to do a job that I haven't done.

Admittedly, it can be a challenge for the boss to maintain the proper authority in the Fun Is Good environment. After all, if employees feel empowered to challenge the status quo and constantly offer ideas, they might get the impression that there's no hierarchy and that everything is open for discussion. But what I've found is that if you give employees freedom, you'll actually have more credibility those times when you do have to say, "We're going to do it this way."

The key is to preserve that Fun Is Good mentality, to maintain the atmosphere that existed when the company was young, the feeling that we're all in this together. The best way to do that is by moving people through the organization.

The other key is to hire people to take your job. If you're a chief and you hire a bunch of wimpy Indians, you're going to be happy in the short term because you can do no wrong—you rule the domain. After a while, though, it's just like looking in the mirror. There's nobody to talk to because it's like talking to yourself. Nobody dares oppose you, and it soon becomes lonely. Isolation destroys the culture of ideas necessary for any organization to succeed.

Instead, find people more talented than you are. Give them credit when they come up with ideas. Take the blame when they fail. Chiefs have to be able to admit when they're wrong. If a chief can walk in and say, "I blew that one," she'll command loyalty.

The problem with most chiefs is that they think, "You will respect me. I am your boss." Employees tune them out. The first time you face your employees and admit that you screwed up, though, it buys tremendous respect.

If the Indian takes the chief's job, then that means the chief keeps ascending. The chief becomes indispensable because he has a reputation for developing talent. The company grows because it's forced to branch out to create jobs for all of these talented people.

The effective chief recognizes that nurturing the Indians doesn't just help them; it helps her. A few years ago, we invited Bill Murray to give the keynote address at the first-ever Veeck Promotional Seminar. Everyone thought he'd get up and tell some wacky stories from his experiences as a minor league baseball owner. Instead, he talked about chiefs and Indians—specifically how as a chief he got all of the credit for movies, yet without the carpenters, makeup people, photographers, and the rest of the staff, the movie could never come together.

Whether it's on the movie set or in the office, there's a huge army of people that has to be moving in one direction.

71

For some chiefs, adjusting to Fun Is Good will be a big transition. You can add a Ping-Pong table or a candy jar; that's easy. The tough part is becoming a chief who brings the Indians into the decision-making process and trains them to take his job.

Here's how you do it: Spend more time worrying about employee perks than your own.

How can you create happier employees?

- Keep as much of the workforce in the informational loop as possible. Stay in touch. Welcome suggestions and contributions and respond quickly.

- Do away with as many form letters and memos as possible. Have a town meeting once a month, and invite everyone in the company.

- Give people freedom. You don't have to turn the office into a playroom. You'll find that people will abuse freedom far less than they'll rebel against a rigid setting.

- Be accessible to employees so they can give suggestions. If you have a company that's spread out on floors, walk up and down a few times a day. If that's not possible, make sure that senior management knows where the pressure points are. If there's a guy in Department A who's having a bad day, make sure somebody is there to give him some of the Fun Is Good attitude.

Creating this attitude is not just important from an internal perspective. If your company is having fun, customers will want to associate with it. People can tell the difference. You know which companies are run by dictators because employees are afraid to make decisions. There's no exchange of information. Employees can't tell customers to have a wonderful day with any degree of sincerity when they're terrified themselves.

Fish rot from the head down, and so do companies. The Fun Is Good atmosphere can start with the Indians, but it helps if the chiefs are on board. It's essential for business. If you're Bill Gates running Microsoft or George Steinbrenner overseeing the New York Yankees, maybe it doesn't matter because you have either a monopoly, a dynasty, or a deck stacked prohibitively in your favor. For everyone else, you need the edge that Fun Is Good brings. A company is kidding itself if it thinks it can be a dysfunctional family internally but project a different image to the customers. It doesn't work that way. People can smell the difference.

However, a harmonious company that blurs the difference between chief and Indian is more likely to project a fun, we're-in-this-together image to its customers. They'll want to be part of the fun, and that's good for business.

. . . .

Fun Is Good Vignette

Chris Sullivan,
Chairman of Outback Steakhouse

"The thing I'm most proud of about the success of Outback Steakhouse is that we've helped more than 200 of our restaurant managers become millionaires. It's just one aspect of our philosophy where we've managed to blur the distinction between chiefs and Indians."

We call these folks our managing *partners*. Each manager of a new Outback Steakhouse, Carrabba's Italian Grill, Bonefish Grill, or any of our other four restaurant concepts is given the opportunity to purchase 10 percent equity in the restaurant for $25,000. We require them to sign 5-year contracts; through this sweat equity arrangement, they become millionaires by the time the restaurant celebrates its 10th anniversary.

More than 95 percent of these restaurant partners are former hourly employees who worked as bartenders, waiters, or kitchen staff. Most complete a second 5-year contract with the store and then decide they want to try a different restaurant concept or perhaps move to a different part of the country.

This program helps us nurture, develop, and retain talented people. If you owned or operated a business for 20 years and were successful, chances are you walked away a millionaire. So instead of teaching these people the business and having them go out and be our competitors, why not be their partners?

We want these people to be able to generate significant net worth. It's tough to accumulate wealth, and we're fiercely proud of the fact we've helped people to do it.

This isn't just altruism; it's vital to the success of our business. As owners, they're more motivated to increase sales and profits. Managers in other companies without ownership stakes don't operate that way. It's a different kind of environment.

We're hardly the only business to provide these sweat equity opportunities, though some companies resist out of fear. They worry about the tax implications, logistics, or what happens if people leave and own a piece of their business. You can work around all of that, and it's never a reason not to do it.

The "Indians" in our company know there are opportunities to move up to ownership level. Even chiefs know they can keep moving up. A managing partner might move up to become responsible for one of our brands in a certain region. That person is responsible for day-to-day operations and putting the management teams together. They help us find sites, acquire real estate, and generally wear multiple hats. You do that for a few years, and suddenly you're ready to be a president of a restaurant concept.

Very few of our managing partners leave, and that's a major reason behind the success of our company, which now has more than 1,000 restaurants worldwide. Our sales volume far exceeds that of other casual steakhouses, largely because of this program and the stability in our restaurants.

Yet we're always changing. It's important to have a corporate culture where ideas are welcomed, encouraged, and easily implemented at every level. It can't be just the chiefs calling the shots from corporate headquarters.

At Outback, we call it a culture of sharing. One of our partners, Jeff Smith, runs a restaurant in Orlando. A few years ago, he noticed that the takeout part of our business was not very effective or enjoyable for everyone involved. It accounted for just 1 or 2 percent of revenue. Customers, especially women, did not like the takeout process. They would pick up the food near the bar area, and this wasn't especially pleasant, especially with kids in tow.

Jeff decided to take the food out to the car. Immediately, takeout business skyrocketed. A couple of our stores in Tampa soon followed suit. Now curbside takeout accounts for more than 10 percent of our business and gives customers the option of patronizing our restaurants even when they don't have time to come inside and dine.

Another one of our managing partners, located in San Antonio, was trying to figure out a way to handle complaints about the long waiting times to get in to eat. Some don't mind; they go to the bar while waiting and make a full evening out of our restaurant. Others don't want to wait.

Having so much business is a nice problem to have, of course, but you always want to find a way to serve the customer better. We had tried call-in seating in other parts of the country, but it never really worked. Our partner in San Antonio figured out an effective system for people to call in reservations and be seated sooner. Call-in seating has been implemented company-wide and has boosted business tremendously.

These are just two of the hundreds of ideas that have been implemented because of this culture of sharing that blurs the distinction between the chiefs and Indians. It's not me or other executives sitting at headquarters and sending out directives. It's listening to the people in the field that are closest to the customers and employees. They know what we have to do next.

People need to have the power to execute ideas on their own. Admittedly, there's a field we play on with certain things we can't go out of bounds on. You can't change the food, labor laws, etc. But as long as you're operating within those parameters, everything else is fair game. Got an idea? Figure out how to pull it off.

When someone finds a solution, give him the credit. People always want to talk to me and Outback cofounders Bob Basham and Tim Gannon, but all we do is tell the stories of what our stars have done. It's like being the owner of a sports franchise: It's your money, but you're not playing the game. Let the stars take the credit.

I love the way Mike tries to break all the rules. Our slogan—"No Rules, Just Right"—gives people the latitude to do what they think is right without getting approvals from 19 different supervisors. They don't have to look it up in a manual. If someone wants to do something and it feels right, who cares about rules? Sometimes things don't work out, but that should never stop you from innovating and letting the ideas flow from every level of the company.

In our business, people have many choices for where they're going to eat, and if we want to generate long-term relationships, we have to accommodate what they want. Customer service is everything.

In 1970, I was managing a restaurant in Rockville, Maryland, and we had a no-substitute rule on the brunch menu. You couldn't substitute one thing for another. One day a customer slipped me a note to see the movie *Five Easy Pieces*, along with a few bucks for the ticket. I went to see the movie, fidgeting in my seat trying to figure out why the customer wanted me to see it. Finally, there's a scene where Jack Nicholson's character tries to cajole a stubborn waitress into bringing him some plain toast after breakfast had stopped being served. It was absurd that she wouldn't give him what he wanted.

I felt like a real jerk, but it's typical of how many restaurant chains operate. We give customers too many rules. We've prevented this at Outback by making "No Rules, Just Right" part of our culture. It started out as a marketing slogan, but it's become more of a principle of our company. Do what seems right, and don't be hung up on chain-of-command, memos, and formalities.

Companies have to get away from this culture of meetings. In many organizations, the leadership just goes to meetings. It's all they do. Everyone needs a vision, but it's not necessarily implemented by having many meetings. We ask our management teams to have one meeting a week and that's it. We have just one meeting a week at headquarters.

I once had a boss in a previous company that made me fly from Tampa to Houston every Monday for a meeting, and I'd come home Tuesday night or Wednesday morning. It was ridiculous, but there were six of us that had to fly in from around the country. It was so unproductive; yet we did this for about a year. I can look back at blocks of my life where there were weeks upon weeks of nothing but meetings for corporate nonsense and I never got out to the restaurants to see anybody. I had no idea what was going on because I was stuck in meetings.

Give people the space to be stars. We have people who have been with us since the beginning, and it's like they're running their own companies. I obviously want to know what's going on, but these people live and breathe it every day. They're the experts. We talk about strategy and share thoughts, but it's not something that has to be done every day. Everyone has autonomy, nobody is micromanaged, and since we pull that off in the corporate office, it takes place in the field. That's our culture.

Our culture is also about giving back to the community. People come to a restaurant to find comfort. We can't always open the restaurant for charitable events, but we can take the food out into the community to help. We can be the catalyst for good things.

We give for the sake of giving, but we know that when you develop relationships with people, you'll be rewarded in the long term. Many companies get involved in the community where headquarters is located, but at Outback, we believe it's equally important for the staff of each store to become active in the community. If community participation is done right, the restaurant partner at each store should be able to get elected mayor.

We also feel responsible to help our young people. Many of them haven't done any community service until they come to work for us. Kids don't seem to be involved as much these days in service clubs and church groups. We have people who have never volunteered in their lives, so we give them the opportunity, and we think that makes people better citizens. Not only that, but they have fun doing it.

Fun Is Good—because it creates an opportunity for people to enjoy themselves every day. You need fun to be able to do anything successfully or on a long-term basis. Fun is what makes me get up excited about work. We've created a culture at Outback where it's a fun place to work.

In 1971, I was finishing college and interviewing for banking jobs. I almost fell asleep in the interviews. I'm not knocking banking, but there wasn't much energy there. I was working in the restaurant industry as a waiter and a bartender and having a blast. Every day was a game. So I quickly gave up on banking and pursued what I thought would be fun.

Fun was a driving principle from the founding of our company. The last thing the world needed was another western-themed steakhouse. Living in the Tampa Bay area, we knew Australia was a popular tourist destination, especially among our retirees. Australia was viewed as a fun, adventurous place. It's consistently rated the place Americans most want to visit abroad. People love Crocodile Dundee, the Sydney Opera House, and the fun-loving attitudes of Australians.

Of course, we had to inject this culture of fun into the company. From the beginning, fun has been one of our five guiding principles, along with quality, sharing, hospitality, and courage. We have disco nights, bowling nights, softball teams—anything that makes the workplace more fun.

Fun is especially important because our hours are long, stressful, and physically demanding. If we didn't have an environment where people knew it was going to be fun, it would never work. When it's Saturday night, the place is packed, and the kitchen is cranking; that's hard work. At the same time, the employees know the people they're working with are fun. There's going to be fun not only at the end of the night but during the shift. At the end of the day, our goal is always to have a great place to work, make money, and have fun.

When people are having fun, they perform better. There's a serious side to everything; in our business, you have to be very serious about delivering quality food in a timely manner. But if you can do this while having fun, you'll be so much better off.

We take great pride at Outback headquarters in not being an uptight environment. The way the jokes and wisecracks fly, you have to have pretty thick skin to work here. But it's effective because the chiefs take just as much abuse as—if not more than—the Indians. Bob Basham and I give each other so much grief, people who don't know us think we must not like each other. I just can't resist pointing out that he has a big bald head. He can't turn down a chance to mention my (lack of) height.

When we founded Outback in 1988, the goal was to build just four or five Outbacks. If that worked, we'd find another restaurant concept. We had no intentions of building a large company, just a nice little business with stores on the west coast of Florida from Gainesville down to Naples.

Instead, our managing partner program and the fun, "no rules" atmosphere drove us beyond our wildest dreams. By blurring the distinction between chiefs and Indians, we created a worldwide operation. More important, we helped hundreds of others become chiefs and fulfill their dreams.

We're All in This Together

One of the key philosophies of our organization is "we're all in this together." It means that everyone pitches in and that nobody is above performing any task, no matter how menial.

It's also a broader view of an organization that eliminates the us-versus-them mentality that pervades so many companies where the chiefs are pitted against the Indians.

Young companies have less trouble pulling this off. Since there are so few people and everyone is struggling to keep the business alive, everyone is pitching in with everything.

But as the company grows, the hierarchy becomes more pronounced. The key is to maintain that attitude of togetherness. When our employees see Bill Murray cleaning up after a concert at one of our parks, they know he's one of them, even if he does own a chunk of the team.

Dad took this to the level of art form. He was the first to show up each day and the last to leave. He was known as a players' owner. Long before free agency, baseball owners treated players like chattel, forcing players to take pay cuts after productive seasons. Dad even spoke out against the reserve clause, which bound players to a single team. He was by design a notoriously poor negotiator, inevitably paying players too much.

His employees loved him. You didn't work *for* Bill Veeck; you worked *with* him.

I applied this philosophy one day in 1994 when the St. Paul Saints players threatened not to show up on an off day to make up a game that had been rained out the night before. They called me into their clubhouse and, for the first time, a Veeck faced a room full of angry players.

The issue wasn't so much the loss of an off day—though they did want an extra $200 per player—so much as it was the buildup of other things. This happens frequently in offices as one minor issue serves as a spark to set off a powder keg that had been slowly building.

I listened to their complaints, which ranged from the legitimate to the exaggerated to the make-believe. I explained that we had to play the game; otherwise, no one would take our independent Northern League seriously. Critics had already suggested it was a beer league full of nobodies, and to cancel a game would destroy our tenuous credibility.

It was a tense, uncomfortable standoff, and I gripped a baseball tightly as I asked the players to work with me to save the game. I offered each of them $75 and left them alone to discuss it.

When I returned 5 minutes later, they still wanted $200. I took a deep breath and spoke from the heart.

"I'm going to acquiesce to your demands, and I imagine when I leave I'm going to be viewed as less than manly. But before I go, I want you to know that I'm doing it because I love this league."

I paused and turned in the direction of Leon "Bull" Durham, a former big leaguer who, like me, had battled substance abuse.

"This league has provided me with a second chance I never thought I'd receive. The same is true for the rest of you. Let's face it. This league is the best thing that's happened not just to me, but to all of us."

With that, I left the clubhouse and walked out to center field for one of the occasional conversations I had with my dad. I gauged his responses by how much the flag moved. Had I compromised my integrity by giving in to the demands?

"Did I do the right thing?" I asked Dad. The flag remained still. A bad sign.

After a half hour, Durham and another player walked out to center field and summoned me back to the clubhouse. Vinny Castaldo, one of the leaders, apparently felt bad about what they had done. They viewed me as a good guy, almost one of their own.

Castaldo said it was not about the money; they just wanted to be heard. They would play the next day, for no additional cash.

The players realized that all of us were in it together and that the front office worked just as hard as they did, even if some of us as owners shared more in the financial success.

By blurring the line between chiefs and Indians, we overcame a mutiny. It's not a stretch to say we saved the league that day. I'd like to think the Saints acted the way they did because they viewed me in the same positive light that Dad's guys did years ago. More likely, they recognized an atmosphere throughout the organization that we were all in this together.

I still have the "mutiny" baseball I gripped through that tense proceeding. It sits in my home office and serves as a reminder to me that we're all in this together.

· ·

FUN IS GOOD

Chapter 3 Summary and Exercises (Chiefs and Indians)

- The way you make a living is directly connected to your soul.
- You don't have to be a chief to change the corporate culture.
- List three things you can do today to make your office or workstation more inviting.
- What can you do to lighten up your office? (Ping-Pong table? Lending library?)
- Does your organization make at least some of its internal documents available to employees? If not, which ones can be made available?
- Keep meetings short, inclusive, and few in number.
- Do Indians become chiefs in your organization? Do you feel like you can move up?
- Hire people to take your job.

Chapter 4

The Human Touch

When did we stop caring? When did we cease to take an interest in the lives of others? Remember all of that talk in the days and weeks following September 11, 2001, about how we'd be more compassionate and altruistic? We'd now have the proper perspective, or so everyone said. Whatever became of that?

There used to be a time when companies referred to employees as *personnel*. That seemed too impersonal, so they came up with the term *human resources*. That's a step in the right direction, though it doesn't seem like we treat employees or coworkers any differently than when we used the military-like term *personnel*.

We all understand the work relationship: You're paid a salary to perform a task. But everyone wants to feel valued. They don't want, in the words of Bob Seger, to feel like a number.

Treating employees and coworkers well isn't just the right thing to do; it's good business. It's amazing how many people work together and don't know the first thing about these people they're toiling alongside.

In addition to Fun Is Good, the second and perhaps only other rule in our organization is that you treat people the way you'd want to be treated. Call it the golden rule, call it hokey or simplistic, but it works.

A few years ago, Linda McNabb, who now is president of our team in Fort Myers, Florida, the Miracle, told me she was having a tough time dealing with her divorce and the impact on her family. It was obvious that this was weighing heavily on her. Before she got too far into it, I told her to take 6 months off.

"Your job will be here when you return. You've cultivated good people who care deeply about you and this team. Everything will be fine."

She was back in 9 days. A cynic might suggest that she was worried that if she stayed away too long, someone else might prove more adept at running that team, but that wasn't the case. Because she was part of a caring atmosphere where she was valued as a person, she felt comfortable coming back quickly knowing that if she needed to take more time off later, she could.

We've had other employees ask if they could work 4 long days a week, either for family or lifestyle reasons. We've tried to be as accommodating as we can, at least during the off-season when our baseball teams don't play 6 or 7 days a week. Since we have six baseball teams, we've allowed people with essentially the same jobs to "trade" cities and relocate because of family considerations.

Most of us spend at least 40 hours a week with coworkers. If we can build strong relationships and personal connections, it creates harmony and makes coming to work more rewarding. We should constantly make an effort to include families in company events.

Regardless of your job description, there are opportunities to show others you care. Take the time to do something special every day. From having a conversation with a coworker to surprising a customer with better-than-expected service to breaking out cookies and milk in the middle of the afternoon, it's the little things that make a difference to you and your colleagues.

We used to have a woman in our organization who brought in delicious baked goods. At the very least, you can purchase doughnuts or bagels for the office. That person becomes an instant hero for brightening the day.

How effectively you interact with coworkers sets the tone for the organization. When people know that colleagues care about their well-being and success, they feel supported. That encourages the free exchange of ideas and innovations. That esprit de corps generates a stronger feeling of accomplishment for the company.

It's also important to extend this caring mentality to customers and clients. When you get to know those you serve and take a sincere interest in their lives and interests, it guarantees better business through strong customer relationships.

Everyone knows what it feels like to be treated exceptionally well, whether it's as a coworker, employee, or customer. Think of how much more fulfilling life would be if people took the time to routinely show others they care. By creating a tightly knit workplace where people care about those they work with and serve, it's easy to build a more fun, respectful, and supportive work environment.

All it takes is a little time. The problem is that we don't have time to do anything. We have all of these allegedly time-saving devices that we didn't have 20 years ago—e-mail, cell phones, the Internet— but instead of giving us more time, they've created an environment in which nothing is a priority.

With Fun Is Good, we bring things back to a reasonable pace. The idea isn't to become so laid back that work is not done and the company does not compete. Instead, it's to acknowledge that time invested applying the human touch is time well invested.

For instance, if there's a woman who has returned to work following maternity leave, she's going to be that much more productive and cheerful if someone takes 10 minutes in the morning to ask about the baby.

If the boss sets the tone for this mentality, it permeates the entire office. If you walk into the kitchen or conference room in your office and the boss is there sipping coffee and chatting about the ball game, that's significant. It does not say that slacking off is okay, just that communication is as important as the two dozen tasks that need to be addressed.

Ask someone if he's busy, and he'll moan and groan, but he can't describe why he's so busy. We don't appreciate what it means to take just 10 minutes to show some genuine concern, except when there's a tragedy or someone dies.

Everyone assumes they follow the golden rule and treat others accordingly, but if you really want to know how you're doing, listen to the first ten things that come out of your mouth each day or in each conversation. If eight of them are complaints or derogatory comments, that says something. People who complain are really talking about themselves.

Think about it. Office gossip and whining has become a national pastime—often literally the way time is passed in the workplace—when it shouldn't be that way. Chitchat is important, but talking about the movie you watched last night is much different than commiserating about someone you feel got an undeserved promotion.

The most popular people in an organization are those who stop and take time for others, utter few critical thoughts, and say little about themselves. Put together a room full of these people and you can accomplish anything.

It's no different than in sports. If you put 12 or 25 or 40 of the most talented athletes in a locker room, you likely never will win the title because there are so many egos and people with the inability to build a team. But give me the same number of players (or employees) with mid-range talent who happen to like each other and are passionate, and we'll reach the mountaintop.

The best way to apply the human touch is to surprise people with kindness. Walk up to someone's workstation and say, "I have two tickets to the concert, and you should be there. Take the rest of the day off."

Managers always tell me this should be done a day beforehand so the worker can be prepared, but I disagree. If you tell them the day before, they'll feel all this pressure to get work done and will stay until midnight the night before; you just create stress.

Don't plan. Be extemporaneous. Let your employees know that you appreciate them. Reward the extra effort.

For instance, we hold concerts in our ballparks. These are major productions, especially for stadium workers already taxed by the grind of a baseball season. There are workers who do not sleep for 2 days in order to pull these concerts off.

That's why we give cash bonuses after concerts. We'll slip $100 in cash to employees to thank them for the extra effort. It's not nearly enough, but it's a sincere gesture of appreciation and an example of an easy way to apply the human touch.

Showing people that you care may not come naturally at first, but once you establish a pattern of taking an interest in others and trying to make their lives easier, it becomes so ingrained you won't even think of it anymore.

Many companies treat employees poorly, paying them just enough to keep them from quitting, figuring they won't take the initiative to find a better situation.

Of course, many employees allow themselves to be treated this way. They'll tolerate a lot of things, but it doesn't have to be like this. The working relationship could be so much better if it's strong at the personal level.

If you're someone who has never taken an interest in coworkers, it's unrealistic to think you're going to change overnight after reading this. But like a new workout regimen, baby steps each day add up to a major change quickly.

We're all works in progress. Even if you've been surly and distant in the past, it's possible to change. People are forgiving, but if you've scared them too many times, they'll naturally be skittish and uneasy in your presence. However, if they see that you're making a sincere effort to change, you'll be amazed at the response. Colleagues will open up far beyond what you've earned or deserved, and it begins to feed on itself.

The idea is to give more than you take out of the office environment. People have made fortunes talking about unconditional love and turning the other cheek, but it's really as simple as giving more than you receive.

There are people who are the recipients of no positive feedback and yet they continue to give. Most of us aren't like that; we need that constant validation.

Now, you might think it's not within your personality or job description to be the person to provide the human touch. But this is not about the office manager sending flowers to the funeral home when a colleague loses a loved one, or providing cake and a nice sendoff when someone leaves.

Those are meaningful, necessary gestures, but applying the personal touch goes further. It's a pattern of consistent behavior displayed by everyone in the workplace.

Here's a simple way to start: The next time someone compiles that employee directory of home addresses and phone numbers, include their birthdays, along with the names of their spouses and children. Throw in *their* birthdays as well.

If everyone has that list posted on his or her desk, it becomes that much easier to acknowledge these noteworthy occasions. So if you still don't think you can apply the personal touch, at least you can do this. It's a start.

The human touch is as simple as building a sense of community in your office. During my time with the Detroit Tigers, we held a series of executive meetings in Lakeland, Florida, and one day we went bowling. I thought it was a silly idea—hey, even I can be stodgy—but it was a blast.

Install a kangaroo court that issues modest fines for goofy behavior. This builds instant solidarity among sports teams who, like office workers, get tired of spending so much time together. The kangaroo court removes some of the tension. Issue $1 fines for any "offense" that you can give colleagues good-natured grief about, whether it's excessive whining, coming back from the deli without soliciting orders from others, or leaving the toilet seat up in the bathroom. Put all of the fines in a jar, and use the proceeds to throw a party.

Company picnics are great, though they seem to be a dying phenomenon. In our business, this is easy to pull off because we control ballparks and can use the fields for barbecues. We end up playing baseball or softball under the lights until 2 a.m. But you don't need to own a ball field; there's no reason any company can't have a picnic. It contributes to that sense of community.

Having board games around is always a good idea. Put out a chess set, Jenga game, or anything that can be played in intervals. Even an uptight law firm—isn't that redundant?—can have a chess set. Buy the deluxe hand-carved model. Whatever you need to fit your pricey décor, just as long as you do something to bring about the sense of community. (Chess is not billable time, however.)

Kids should be welcome. Let kids come to work for a day. Not that phony "shadow" program where kids just sit in a corner playing video games on the computer, but give them meaningful jobs. They can deliver mail, run errands, and make copies. Older kids can walk around and sit in on meetings. Have children answer the phones. My daughter has been doing this for our teams since she was 7 years old. We've probably violated some child labor laws, but who cares as long as she's having fun?

Having kids around changes the entire office dynamic. People stop using foul language and griping under their breath. Not only that, but it's good for business.

You don't think so? When a kid answers the phone, it disarms the caller. The adult on the other end wants to know who is on the phone and it places callers in a good mood. It casts your company in a good light. Most kids can transfer calls and take messages.

We've gone so far as to have kids run our entire operation for a day. We turned the running of our club in Ft. Myers, Florida, over to children for one game. They directed traffic in the parking lot, with cars parked everywhere, and did everything but sell beer and run deep fryers at the concession stands. We appointed corporate officers, assigned public address announcers—everything.

It was a roaring success. People would wait in line for 2 extra minutes while the kids counted change. Eventually they'd give up and tell the kids to keep the change. We never made so much at the concession stands. Major League Baseball, which often scoffs at minor league ideas, was quick to embrace this promotion and called it "Kids' Opening Day."

. . . .

Customer Karma

Take the time to get to know your customers. You never know whom you might meet.

During the early days of the St. Paul Saints, I'd strike up a conversation with a wheelchair-bound fan who attended many of our games. We had a mutual love of rock and roll, and I'd tell him about the concerts I had staged at Comiskey Park in Chicago and in minor league ballparks.

The man's name was Larry Kegan, and he loved coming out to Saints games. I mentioned that I had been a huge fan of Bob Dylan growing up but that I never booked him for a show because I was afraid he'd turn out to be a jerk. Now, Bob Dylan was no more likely to be a jerk than anyone else, but for some reason I didn't want to take a chance on shattering the image I had created.

Larry nodded and we turned our attention back to the game.

The following March, team attorney Tom Whaley and Tom Mischke, a radio talk show host in the Twin Cities, arranged for me to meet Bob Dylan backstage at a concert around the time of my 43rd birthday. Larry Kegan had made it possible by writing Dylan a letter about a diehard fan that ran a minor league baseball team in St. Paul.

It turned out that Larry Kegan was a childhood friend of Robert Zimmerman, who became Bob Dylan. The two had met as teenagers at summer camp and maintained a close friendship. In 1978, Dylan dedicated his album "Street Legal" to Kegan, a singer-songwriter who later performed on stage with Dylan, Jackson Browne, and others.

Kegan was a remarkably accomplished guy despite enduring a diving accident that left him a paraplegic at age 15 and a car accident that rendered him a quadriplegic a decade later. He ran a resort for disabled veterans in Mexico, managed orange groves in Florida, and sang at Governor Jesse Ventura's inaugural celebration in Minnesota in 1999. Larry performed at American Indian functions—and even at Stillwater Prison.

That concert where I met Bob Dylan was one of the few times I've been rendered speechless. I literally could not say anything to Dylan.

"You're the baseball guy," Dylan said in that unmistakable voice. "I love baseball. You've got that stadium with the train. I love trains."

A few years later, Bob Dylan played a concert at Midway Stadium, home of our St. Paul Saints. My fears were unfounded; he turned out to be a wonderful guy. I even went backstage and talked to Dylan with Bill Murray, which has to rank as one of the more surreal moments anyone could hope to experience.

I'd like to think the fun experience we provided Larry Kegan at Midway and the pleasant chats we enjoyed inspired him to do this special thing for me.

Larry died of cardiac arrest in 2001 while driving his van. He was 59. I'll always be grateful for my friendship, however brief, with Larry because he taught me an enduring lesson.

If you take the time to show a genuine interest in people, whether it's coworkers, customers, or simply those you meet serendipitously, you never know where it might lead.

Sometimes the most unlikely people can fulfill your dreams.

• •

Take the time to get to know your coworkers. You never know what you'll discover. In St. Paul, there's a woman named Connie Rudolph whose job description includes serving as groundskeeper for Midway Stadium, home of our Saints baseball team.

If you were to approach Connie as just a groundskeeper, you'd get a woman who is an expert on dirt and grass and knows how to maintain a beautiful ballfield.

But if you get to know her, you'll find there's so much more. She's a voracious reader, an excellent cook, and an all-around creative person who brings a lot more to her job than just knowledge of sod. She creates elaborate designs in the outfield grass by the way she mows. Fans appreciate those extra touches. She doesn't have to do it, but she does not only because she's the consummate professional but also because she feels like part of our family.

Though Connie works for the city and is not employed by the Saints, we'd gladly hire her. Other companies might remain distant from a city official assigned to them, let alone get to know her on a personal level. But that's not how we operate, and our organization is the better for it.

Another key member of our family is Andy Nelson. In the early days of the St. Paul Saints, Andy used to hang out at the stadium even when the team wasn't playing. No one was quite sure why. He was a quiet guy, always clad in work clothes and, on the surface, I suppose, a little odd.

Once we took the time to get to know him, we discovered another amazing person. Andy had worked as a newspaper editor, which probably explains his nocturnal nature. He's a gifted artist, and we put him to work designing program covers and painting elaborate murals throughout our ballpark. Many stadiums have imitated us by installing murals, and Andy is the reason for this national phenomenon.

No matter what your business, there are people dying to become part of your operation. Often we look at them as annoyances, like houseguests who won't go away. But if you scratch the surface, you'll find there's something wonderful in these people. As a society, we don't take the time to do this, to find out what a person is all about. If you look deeper, you'll find that your employees are tremendous resources. The more you get to know them, the more you'll benefit. Before you hire outside help or additional employees, make sure you're tapping into all of those human resources you have in front of you.

· ·

Found in Translation

A few years ago, the F/X cable network approached the St. Paul Saints with the idea of producing a season-long documentary on the team. This was in 1996, long before anyone used the term "reality television." Rupert Murdoch didn't yet have Major League Baseball to put on his cable network, so he needed something cheap and relatively entertaining.

In 1996, the Saints were 3 years old, a "mature business," you could say. We didn't need publicity the way we had in the early days. Still, I was intrigued. I don't know much about the television business, even though my parents once hosted their own show and I've hosted a number of programs as well. As far as negotiating, I wasn't exactly in a position of strength.

These slick TV guys from Los Angeles probably figured they could take advantage of our little Podunk operation in St. Paul. Fortunately, I turned to the one person in our organization who knew something about TV.

I called Bill Murray, and for 45 minutes he explained how the television business worked. He said the TV guys would come in and tell us we'd sell 8 million hats and T-shirts because of the show and we should be thankful not to be paying them for the exposure. They would come in with their lawyers and hardball us.

"Tell them you'll take $7,500 an episode," Murray said. "They'll tell you to go (bleep) yourself and hang up the phone, but they'll settle for $5,000."

Murray also said I needed to come up with some other demands. "If you act like you're grateful for all of this and accept their line that you're going to sell lots of hats, they're going to treat you accordingly."

Like Dad, I've been accused of being a terrible negotiator. I tend to be too nice. Murray said I needed to show these guys that I was a serious businessman. Otherwise, they'd treat me like that naive guy.

I mentioned that I could use a 5-minute video on our operation that employees could take when they go out to speak to groups. I'd also like a similar tape to show to prospective clients, and a third video—a season highlight film—we could sell at the souvenir stands.

"That's good," Murray said. Then he lowered his voice. "This filming isn't going to be easy. After 2½ months of this, your most good-natured employees are going to be in one another's faces. Envy will raise its head, and someone will be upset because he's not getting enough screen time. People will be arguing and creating frictions that never existed. And no matter what F/X tells you, the cameras *will* be intrusive."

Things unfolded exactly as Murray had predicted, especially the negotiations.

Tom Whaley, our attorney, told the F/X people we wanted $7,500 an episode. They told Tom to go (bleep) himself and hung up.

A few days later, an executive showed up in St. Paul in an expensive suit and wingtips. I was wearing sneakers and a shirt with a Saints logo. (I have few shirts that don't have logos on them.) We sat in the empty stadium.

"You know," the executive said. "When this series comes out, you guys are going to sell a lot of hats and T-shirts."

I bit my lip, stifling a laugh, and nodded. We got our $5,000 an episode, along with our additional films. The cameras were intrusive and there were some flare-ups among employees, but F/X did a great job. You still sometimes can catch reruns of the show late at night. I guess Rupert never came up with enough programming.

Our last game of the '96 season was in Fargo, and afterward everyone, including the F/X people, ended up in a bar to toast the end of the championship campaign. The same executive sat down with my wife, Libby.

"Your husband is a notoriously lousy negotiator," he said. "How did he know exactly what to ask for?"

Libby smiled. "Do you think Bill Murray learned anything from all those years of *Saturday Night Live*?"

If you want to negotiate a great deal, find an expert. Otherwise, someone will view you the way that executive looked at us: like a bunch of yokel Midwesterners who fell off a grain wagon. They'll underestimate your people, but that's okay. Take advantage of it.

Chances are you have that expert working for you already. In this instance, we had an obvious resource in Bill Murray. There have been other times when Andy Nelson has been that person—or one of our interns. The Detroit Tigers have a guy who runs the mailroom who is one of the most knowledgeable people I've ever met. If you want to know anything about the Tigers, he's one-stop shopping.

If you get to know everything about the people working for you, your company will be so much better off and your employees will be motivated to put all of their skills to work.

· ·

We've developed this notion in corporate America that it's unprofessional to take an interest in the lives of our coworkers and customers. Why is that? This isn't about being nosy; it's about taking a genuine interest in people. If someone says you're prying or it's none of your business, fine. At least then you know that that person is unapproachable.

There's no inherent professional conflict in caring for people. There's nobody who isn't flattered by someone's taking an interest in them. If your kid has been sick, you'll be touched if a coworker asks how the little one is doing—or better yet, lets you take off early to tend to the child.

It's that simple, and we're all capable of it. Whenever there's a natural disaster or tragedy, people open up their wallets and send money to people they don't know. They bring strangers into their homes. Yet we often ignore people we know well who require nothing more than a few expressions of interest.

A few years ago, my daughter, Rebecca, appeared on the TV program *Inside Edition,* which chronicled her dealings with retinitis pigmentosa. When the show aired, the Foundation Fighting Blindness was inundated with donations.

We have an inherent need to be part of this community of man, and the workplace is an extension of that community that begins at home. You can't divide your life into compartments and say, "I'm going to care only about people in these situations."

It's the same way with running a business. If you think you can operate a company in a dictatorial fashion and presume that your company will come across as some sort of warm-and-fuzzy outfit that caters to its customer, you're crazy. Employees always betray something.

If you have a workplace where employees have a good time and care about one another, on the other hand, it's infectious. Customers want to be a part of it. They spend more money, tell others about you, and it filters throughout the organization, resulting in increased revenues.

One of the greatest assets a company can have is that it projects enthusiasm and caring behavior that affirms the customer's decision to do business with it. The customers want to pat themselves on the back for being smart enough to choose this business partner.

If you're an employee, make it a point to let your colleagues and managers know of any outside interests you have that might help the company. People tend to get pigeonholed, and everyone forgets that well-rounded background listed on the résumé that might have contributed to the hiring in the first place.

Just as employers need to get to know employees, the employee needs to find out more about the employer or supervisor. This isn't about brown-nosing or sucking up. Everyone needs a mentor; we'll discuss that more in Chapter 11.

Instead of just taking a paycheck out of a job, take precious insider knowledge that will help you build a career. Taking an interest in others and applying the human touch is the right thing to do. If all that happens is you make someone else's life a little more enjoyable, then you've succeeded.

You might also find that applying the human touch can boost your career in ways you never thought possible.

• •

Fun Is Good Vignette

Annie Huidekoper,
"Life Coach"

"I spent four seasons working for the St. Paul Saints. I probably never will work in such a Fun Is Good environment ever again, but I know the mindset applies everywhere because I've employed it in some of the most depressing places imaginable, environments in dire need of the human touch."

My degree is in health administration and planning. I've spent much of my career working in stressful, disheartening places such as cancer clinics and "natural health centers," which seriously ill people turn to when conventional medicine has not worked. In both instances, you're dealing with folks in desperate need of hope—or at least some good cheer.

People need to laugh, and you don't have to be naturally funny or know a bunch of good jokes. Part of it is simply helping people feel comfortable and relaxed. Listen. Tell stories. Poke fun at yourself. Be there for people.

There's nothing more intimidating or frustrating than being hospitalized. Often, people just need someone to talk to, and though there's rarely anything funny about the situation, laughter is critical.

I created a program called the "condition of the month." Each month, I'd "honor" an ailment such as osteoporosis, menopause, or the flu. We'd make posters, hold workshops, and generally band together to eradicate this ailment. It wasn't a big deal, but it brought people together—we even opened it to the public—and we found ways to laugh at things that you don't think of as funny.

Laughter is contagious, which was the motto of Patch Adams, the wacky doctor portrayed by Robin Williams in the hit movie a few years back. Like Adams, I believe in the healing power of laughter because I've seen firsthand how effective it can be. If it can heal, imagine what it can do to transform a sluggish workplace. After all, it's not just the ill who need the human touch.

For several years, I worked as an "interior plant technician," which is a fancy way of saying I went around to office complexes with a lot of indoor greenery and took care of the plants. Such people usually go unnoticed by workers as they hustle through their days; they blend in with the landscape.

I made it a point to greet people with a hello and a smile. I went about my inherently boring job in a cheerful manner. In a small way, I helped brighten the days of a few people and, if nothing else, gave them an appreciation for the job my company did in adding some life to their workplaces. Maybe you know of a doorman or janitor who always seems to be in a cheerful mood despite a job description that seems downright miserable. If they can be upbeat, I figured, why couldn't I?

When I moved on to another job, managers from several of the offices I handled called my employer to ask about me. A few wondered how they'd ever replace me, a remarkable sentiment considering people probably never before noticed the interior plant technician or even realized their companies employed such a person.

These days, I work as a "life coach," helping people caught in a career rut rediscover—or discover for the first time—what makes them happy and how they can find joy and passion in their careers. I try to help these people identify what brings them joy and chart a path toward finding it. In short, I'm showing them how to find Fun Is Good.

So many workplaces have become sterile. Even if we have no feelings for our colleagues, we still have that need for connection. It's okay to talk about something other than work and find out what makes people tick. Laughter is not only permissible; it's essential. Without the human touch, a workplace is a terribly depressing place.

• •

Before we move on to the next section, let's take a moment and define five ways to bring Fun Is Good to your workplace. They can be simple things, like greeting people more often, or something ambitious such as a wacky promotion.

If you're looking to move to another job or career, list five things you feel passionate about, and craft a career around those interests. What is your ideal gig? Try to match your interests with a career, not vice versa.

In our organization, we ask everyone to create a personal marketing plan that projects where they want to be next year, 3 years down the road, and 5 years from now. They share it with me. Try to implement such a program in your office. If nothing else, do it yourself.

I believe strongly in writing down goals and lists. I do it constantly, especially when I'm on planes, waiting for planes, or just have some downtime. Some of the most successful companies have been launched on cocktail napkins and scraps of paper, but find a decent place to write *these* goals down. Studies suggest that people who write down goals accomplish more. It forces you to focus and, in a small way, is a sign of commitment.

Now that we've established those goals, let's examine the mindset needed to bring them to life.

So go ahead. Write them down on paper or type them into a computer. Make them ambitious but specific. If it's the end of the year, call it a priority list for the new year.

Post the list on your desk, if you like, but at least reference the goals every so often. You'll be pleasantly surprised by your progress.

FUN IS GOOD

Chapter 4 Summary and Exercises (The Human Touch)

- Treat coworkers the way you would wish to be treated.
- Get to know your coworkers on a personal level. Camaraderie makes work fun.
- Get to know your customers on a personal level. You'll be amazed at the benefits.
- Tap into the talents of your staff, not just those that fit the job description. They can help in ways you never considered.
- What are three small things you can do in the next week to show people you care?
- Define five ways you can bring Fun Is Good to your workplace.
- Incorporate children into your workplace culture. It keeps the office young.
- Surprise colleagues and employees with kindness and random time off.
- Appoint a kangaroo court in the office to keep the atmosphere loose.
- Write a personal marketing plan.

Part II

· · · · · · · · · · · · · · ·

Lighten Up

NOW THAT YOU'VE found your passion, changed your attitude, and applied the human touch to your career and workplace, let's look at specific ways to bolster your career and business with this new philosophy. We'll examine how my dad, Bill Veeck, employed Fun Is Good in his daily routines and see how the philosophy is something that can improve not just your workplace and career but every aspect of your life. We'll examine the power of irreverence and how it can shape careers and businesses. We'll show how laughter is not only good business but also the best way to deal with adversity.

Chapter 5

Lessons from Dad

D ad had a lot to say. Several books were written about him, and he cranked out three books himself. Dad spent a lot of ink railing against the baseball establishment—and with good reason. We won't revisit those battles. Instead, I'll use this chapter to explain how the people skills, outlook, and customer service strategies of baseball's greatest innovator apply to the modern workplace.

More important, we'll examine how Dad *lived*. He never lost that childhood fascination with anything new. Dad slept little because he was afraid he'd miss something. He was a voracious reader, and his personal skills were unmatched. He was a true Renaissance man, able to talk with some degree of expertise on almost anything, but what made him remarkable was his willingness to listen to people.

If you study Bill Veeck simply as a gonzo marketer, you're missing much of the man's genius. There's so much more to be learned from him about how to embrace life, challenges, and, most important, people.

I challenge you to find a sad Bill Veeck story. Not a poignant one or a moving one, but a sad one. You won't find it. My dad lost his right leg below the knee as a result of a Marine Corps training accident, underwent 36 surgeries, and had to soak the stump of his right leg for hours every day. Yet he refused to admit he was handicapped—just "crippled." He even poked fun at his ailment, especially when he'd phone or visit recent leg amputees. These people were just devastated by what had taken place. But within minutes, Dad would have them laughing.

"The only things we have to fear are fire and termites," he'd say. "Our feet only get half as cold. Our socks go twice as far."

"Maybe I'll meet someone without a left leg," he'd say. "We could buy shoes together."

The only immortality we have is when someone says, "I know a guy who did it this way." Dad died nearly 20 years ago, and it's like he's still here because of what he instilled in me—and so many others.

Dad's lessons apply to any business, and they're even more applicable today because so many companies have lost any notion of customer service and creating fun in the workplace.

Many people have tried to crystallize Dad's philosophies. Mom did the best job in 1991, when she gave a speech on the occasion of Dad's posthumous induction into Baseball's Hall of Fame. I've borrowed from her speech, along with my own experiences and those of others who worked with him, to apply his teachings to Fun Is Good.

Lesson 1: It's All about the Customer

Dad created a carnival atmosphere in his ballparks, to the point where he'd occasionally bring in circus elephants. He was fascinated by the spectacle of the circus and once tried to purchase one. He wanted fans to expect the unexpected and believed that "every day is Mardi Gras, and every fan is king."

However, Dad resented it when people called him "the P. T. Barnum of baseball" because it implied that, like Barnum, he believed there was a sucker born every minute. Nothing could have been further from the truth.

Dad understood the value of customer service long before companies spent millions on research and consultants to help improve it. During a game, he'd move through the ballpark, soliciting opinions from fans. "You don't own a business," he'd tell employees. "You're just the caretaker."

When was the last time you walked through a store and had an employee ask your opinion of something? For most people, the answer is never. Customer service is more than just asking, "May I help you?" It's a genuine back-and-forth relationship whereby you try to constantly give the customer more.

I dare you to try to get the CEO of a company on the phone. Call a switchboard and asked to be patched through. You can't do it. Dad took calls, though. He was relentless in pursuit of opinions. We never had an unlisted home phone number. "You never know who might call," he'd say. If you called one of his teams and asked to speak to Bill Veeck, that's who you got on the phone.

"The switchboard operator isn't going to ask who you are or what you want," he'd say. "The next voice you hear is going to be mine."

Sure, there were times when it was inconvenient or disruptive, but Dad maintained that it made him sharper. Information was a two-way street, and by keeping the lines of communication open, he learned more, and his business benefited because he knew what the customers wanted.

When the owner of a company is that accessible, customers become more loyal. Dad always gave the impression that he was winking at the fans, as if we were all in on some great joke. That's easy to pull off when you know many of your customers personally.

Now, you might suggest that times have changed and it's more difficult to be accessible, especially if you're not in the public limelight like Bill Veeck was. I disagree. With e-mail and cell phones, it's never been easier to stay in touch. There's no reason you, Ms. CEO, can't take at least a few of your calls personally, is there?

There's nothing more disarming to an angry caller than when the president takes the phone. They're expecting to hear from some operator in a call center that has only a loose affiliation with the company. Instead, they get The Big Cheese on the line. Granted, they might lay into you, but so what? Chances are, you can help that customer, and if you do, you'll no doubt have a very loyal one. Not only that, but that person likely will tell 10 others.

Is there any reason you can't offer that kind of accessibility at least once a week?

There's no more important person in your organization than the one who answers the phones. That person provides the first impression of a company. Dad recognized this long before the so-called corporate experts came up with terms like "pressure points" or "touch points." He understood that it made a big difference when the phone was answered, "Good afternoon, Chicago White Sox, how may I help you?" instead of "White Sox."

Dad hired people from the phone company to work for his teams because nobody was more equipped to handle angry callers. Those people have heard it all—complaints about the service, the equipment, the bill—and sometimes it got personal. These callers were ticked off and would attack the phone employees personally.

So, after dealing with that, it was easy for them to come to work in baseball. You don't like your seat? No problem. We'll find you another one.

Customer service has become a lost art. Plenty of companies have gone under—not because they didn't have good products or strong management, but because they placed little importance on customer service.

It all starts with how you answer the phone.

Lesson 2: It's Not about You

In 1999, *Chicago* magazine published a wonderful article on Dad's relationship with his children.

The editors at *Chicago* were fascinated by the notion that even though Bill Veeck had led a very public life, little was known about his relationship with his kids, with the possible exception of the one problem child who kept coming up with goofy stunts in minor league baseball.

Dad gave countless interviews. Some of his best friends were sportswriters. Mom had been a publicist for the Ice Capades. Dad wrote newspaper columns and magazine articles, appeared on regular radio programs, and my parents hosted television and radio programs. They were about as accessible as two people could be.

And yet, little was known about the six children they had together or the three that he had from his first marriage.

Dad was protective of his family life—and us—but there was something else at work.

Even though he wrote three books, they were more his thoughts on baseball, business, and life than they were autobiographies. Dad had no interest in talking about himself. He knew his own story and didn't need to live it again. Instead, he viewed everyone else's story as much more interesting than his own. With that attitude, every day became a new adventure, and his ability to expand his horizons was unlimited.

We're all told at a young age that there's a reason we have two ears and only one mouth. Unfortunately, we spend our lives acting as if we need to use the mouth twice as much to even the score.

Dad recognized that we glean so much from the lives of others. Dad could talk for half an hour with someone he'd just met at the corner saloon.

We've already discussed how important it is to apply the human touch, to take an interest in the lives of your workers. Dad took it a step further by going into business with his friends. Some might say that's a dangerous thing, but his position was that if you're going to spend so much time with people, why not spend it with your friends?

Dad's memory was sharp in part because his mind was not clogged with his own self-absorbed thoughts. Once you can distance yourself from that and take an interest in the lives of others, you'll be amazed at how much you can learn.

Lesson 3: Keep It Clean

Whenever you're expecting company, you go through heroic efforts to scrub everything in the house. You want everything to look just right so guests don't think of you as a slob. More important, you want them to leave with a positive impression of you and your home.

Yet why is it companies don't take the same approach? It's amazing how often we're subjected to disgusting restrooms in restaurants, offices, stadiums, and movie theaters. Or we pull into a parking lot that hasn't been repaved in decades. The shrubs are dead, the lobby hasn't been updated in 30 years, and the focal point of the entryway is a cigarette sandbox.

That sure leaves me with a positive first impression!

Dad understood that you needed to show the same respect for your customers that you did your houseguests—even more so because friends and family tend to be more forgiving than paying customers. If you keep things as clean as you would your home, it shows respect, and people will spend more.

Customers judge your business long before they ever meet you. It starts with the parking lot and the reception area, but there's perhaps nothing more important than having a clean, organized business—including the bathrooms. It's all part of an approach to your business, and it says something about the people running it and the respect that you have for your customers.

When you have a nasty bathroom, it says that you're cutting corners and taking customers for granted. This isn't the case in just the restaurant business. If you run a dirty building, it doesn't matter how good your customer service is because all anyone is going to remember is the filth.

Restaurants with dirty bathrooms scare me. People using these bathrooms handle my food. If this is how the bathroom is kept, why should I think the kitchen will be any better?

It's not just the bathroom. Take a look at the reception area, the conference rooms—everything. Don't blame the owner of your building for not updating the place. Take it upon yourself to do so. (If you are the owner of the building, you have no excuse.)

Even if you can't afford to rebuild or renovate, you can repaint. Whenever Dad took over a new ballpark, he had the place scrubbed and repainted until it sparkled. He recognized that cleanliness and an inviting atmosphere were especially important to women, so he installed soft lighting and full-length mirrors in the ladies' rooms.

Assign someone to remove graffiti on a daily basis. If you place framed art on the walls in the bathrooms, you're less likely to have vandalism. Even those framed advertisements over urinals add to the ambience—and provide revenue. (It all makes a difference, though I can tell you from running facilities for years that graffiti is just as prevalent in the women's room as in the men's.)

Any building or workplace can be spruced up. I know because we took one of the homeliest concrete slabs of a stadium and made it into something special in St. Paul. We scrubbed and painted. We planted flowers everywhere, installed hanging planters where dirt didn't exist, and, with the direction of Andy Nelson, painted murals throughout the ballpark. We painted the bathrooms, hung artwork, and kept them immaculate. Our customers now think of Midway Stadium as a warm and inviting place.

People should be cleaning constantly. I never get upset when I walk into a bathroom and half of it has been cordoned off by someone cleaning. That shows me that someone cares.

We've sent employees to Disney World just to see how the place is kept clean. Now, I'm not a huge fan of some of the ways Disney operates. Why a parent would want to spend big money at a place where each ride spits you out inside a gift shop is anyone's guess.

But that's my personal beef; the company sets the standard for cleanliness. Nothing is ever out of place at a Disney theme park. There are people cleaning constantly and though you're aware of them, they're not in your face. It takes an impressive effort to keep that place clean given the thousands of people that trample through each day, spilling soda and ice cream, tossing cigarette butts, and generally acting like inconsiderate tourists.

When you're going to charge the prices Disney does, you had better set the standard for cleanliness. That doesn't mean everyone else is off the hook.

If you pull into a neatly landscaped parking lot and walk through a lobby full of flowers, you're predisposed to having a good feeling about a company and more likely to do business.

It's not just business owners who have to follow these standards. Keeping workspaces clean and orderly not only gives the proper impression but also makes you more productive.

I know I can work twice as hard as anyone because I'm prepared at the end of the day to start the next. I clear the desk, put everything away, and know where to begin the following day. If you make lists and know what to do the next morning, you can hit the ground running instead of spending the first 45 minutes trying to figure out where to begin.

It's so much easier if you keep things clean. You owe it to your customers—and yourself.

Lesson 4: Laugh at Adversity

Dad used to refer to himself as the bionic man. "I'm half-blind, can't hear, have just one leg, and the other one doesn't work so well," he'd say. "And it's a beautiful day."

That could serve as his epigraph. He was the eternal optimist; that was the only way he knew to approach life. He understood that you had to enjoy each day no matter how bad things seemed.

Dad was hardly the first or the last to use baseball as a metaphor for life, but few have pegged it as accurately as he did. When you go to a ballpark, there's a pretty good chance your team is going to lose. At certain points during Dad's tenure as a baseball owner, there was a *very* good chance his team was going to lose.

Yet he was determined to make sure his customers had a great experience, even if they were having an otherwise lousy day or the product itself (the team) was losing. That was one of his guiding principles: Enjoy each day no matter what challenges you face. How could you not be inspired by a guy like Bill Veeck? He spent the hours of 5 to 8 a.m. soaking his stump in Epsom salts so he could make it through the day. He wore thick glasses to correct his poor vision and hearing aids because he had lost some of his hearing by contracting jungle rot while in the service.

Yet nothing slowed him down. He possessed a boundless energy that came from the time he spent recuperating from the initial loss of his leg. He spent that year productively, reading books, but vowed that once he got out of that bed, he was going to make the most of his time.

Dad lived on roughly 3 hours of sleep a night for years at a time, in part because he had to get up to soak his stump, but also because he didn't want to miss anything. Between the ballgames, the saloons, and every conversation in between, he squeezed as much into 71 years as anyone could.

Dad wasn't supposed to make it to 50. When he owned the White Sox, from 1959 to 1961, he began experiencing blackouts and persistent headaches. Doctors at the Mayo Clinic told him he had better sell the team and take it easy. They thought he had brain cancer or some other terminal illness. He moved us to the Eastern Shore of Maryland, where he began putting his affairs in order for the inevitable.

Of course, Dad wasn't ready to die, no matter what the doctors said. He lived another 25 years. He spent the 1960s writing newspaper columns and magazine articles, appearing on television shows, and becoming active in the Civil Rights movement. In the late '60s, he ran the Suffolk Downs racetrack in Boston, where he came up with such promotions as the Ben Hur Handicap (a chariot race) and the Lady Godiva Handicap, an all-female-jockey race that Dad billed as "Eight Fillies on Eight Fillies."

In 1975, he reacquired the White Sox and the circus reopened for business. Even after he sold the team in 1981, he continued to take the pulse of the fans, at least those in the Wrigley Field bleachers, where he spent many afternoons in his latter years.

Not bad for a guy with a collection of ailments who was supposed to have died long before Woodstock. I'm convinced that when he finally passed, he waited until January 2 just so he could see what the New Year of 1986 would bring.

Dad died of a heart attack, but the *Washington Post* sportswriter Tom Boswell had a better explanation. "Cause of Death: Life."

Nancy Faust, the longtime organist for the Chicago White Sox, believed Dad actually lived much longer. "With the amount of sleep he didn't get, Bill probably died at 85 instead of 71."

The single most important element of any career, assuming there's a passion for it, is the ability to handle adversity. What matters most is how you deal with those challenges internally.

If you externalize it, it starts looking like the most terrible thing in the world. For years, I looked at Disco Demolition as the end of my life. I had a chance and I blew it. It was easy to look at my situation like a mountain I couldn't climb.

The real mountain is forgiving yourself, and the key is to persevere: to dust yourself off, try another approach, and eventually succeed. We have this idea that we've been knocked down so many times, *we* must be the problem. Once you become less egocentric in your decision-making and the way you view things, you'll be a lot better off. It's as simple as saying, "I've joined a great club: a group of amazing people that overcame major failures."

There's a silver lining in anything. Not long after we began writing this book, I fell off a bicycle and broke my right femur in three places. I had been cruising through the neighborhood and had seen some kids shooting hoops. They'd tossed me the ball and I'd attempted to execute a shot from the bike.

I'd forgotten that I was not 12 anymore. I took a nasty spill, spent several days in the hospital as doctors put my leg back together, and was confined to the house for weeks. For someone who travels for business as much as I do, this was a major setback.

The injury forced me to realize that I wanted to spend more time at home anyway, and that I didn't want to maintain such a rigorous travel schedule that kept me away from my family. I could do most of my work via e-mail and the phone. I became more focused on this book.

Granted, I quickly grew weary of friends making wisecracks about "another one-legged Veeck" and that by shattering my *right* leg, I was taking my emulation of Dad a little too far. On a positive note, the injury gave me some fresh material for speeches.

Laugh at adversity. It's the only way to deal with it.

Lesson 5:
Never Lose Your Childhood Curiosity

One of the great joys of parenting is dealing with youngsters who have just discovered how to use the word "why." "Why?" becomes their response to every explanation, no matter how succinctly you answered the previous question.

Bill Veeck never stopped asking why—or why not? If told something couldn't be done, he'd ask why not.

At some point in our lives, we lose that childlike curiosity. We become jaded or cynical. Maybe we've been told "that's the way it is" so often we quit asking.

Dad never got that way. His mind was constantly churning, in part because he kept getting ideas from others by taking an interest in their lives. He used to keep a pad of paper near the bed so that when he had an idea in the middle of the night—during that rare time he slept—he could scribble it down.

When you maintain that childlike curiosity, you develop a mental edge. You see things differently. Dad once served as a consultant for the National Bohemian Breweries, and one of the first things he asked was why beer did not come in square cans.

Sound ridiculous? Think about it. If beer cans were square like milk cartons instead of cylindrical, you could get 25 percent more beer in them. As it is, a lot of space is wasted when beer is packed and transported.

The folks at National Bohemian researched the matter and gave it some consideration before concluding that Dad's proposal was impossible. Unlike cylinders, square beer cans would not roll down conveyor belts. The costs of retooling were astronomical.

You might argue that this was not childlike curiosity so much as it was the natural inspiration of a man who spent a lot of time with a can of beer in his hand. But this was typical Bill Veeck.

Perhaps it helped that Dad had good genes. His maternal grandfather was Lee De Forest, who patented more than 300 inventions, including the vacuum tube. My great-grandfather's inventions were essential to the development of voice transmission, long-distance radio, and eventually television.

It's almost eerie how things Dad thought of have come to fruition. In baseball, he lobbied for years, like his father before him, on behalf of interleague play, which would pit American League teams versus their National League counterparts during the regular season. The purists howled, though the concept finally was adopted for 1997, 64 years after my grandfather had proposed it.

Dad always wanted to combine a bookstore and a coffee shop. These days, it's tough to find a bookstore without a coffee shop. Borders and Barnes & Noble have become retail giants. He even thought of having a bookstore/coffee shop attached to a greenhouse, figuring well-read people tended to like flowers. Who knows? Maybe we'll see that concept marketed within the next 10 years.

When I was about 9, Dad came home with a little box. Dad was like Gepetto, the toymaker who created Pinocchio. He was always coming up with ideas.

As he opened the box, he said, "This is going to make baseball more fun."

Inside the box was a little scoreboard with pinwheels. It sang the "Hallelujah" chorus and exploded with brilliant flashes of light. My parents had gone to see William Saroyan's play *The Time of Your Life*, which featured a closing scene in a saloon where a pinball machine explodes.

Dad thought it was a perfect metaphor for a home run.

"Do you know what the most amazing thing about this scoreboard is?" he asked. "I'm building it with someone else's money."

Dad had contacted dozens of companies he thought might be interested in sponsoring the exploding scoreboard. They either laughed at him or refused to hear his proposal. But a woman who ran the marketing for Union 76, the gasoline company, grasped the magic behind the invention.

The other baseball owners scoffed in 1960 when Dad unveiled the "monster exploding scoreboard," with its pinball design and fireworks after each home run. Players and fans, of course, loved it, and similar scoreboards were built throughout baseball.

Dad never stopped looking at things through the eyes of a child. He liked having young people around, not simply because it enabled him to mentor and teach others but because it brought fresh ideas to the organization. I'm not sure to what degree Dad grasped the power of rock 'n' roll, but he understood that the concerts I staged boosted attendance. For better or for worse, he gave me the freedom to stage Disco Demolition.

Keep asking "why not?" Long before I worked for Dad, he was the first to stage post-game fireworks celebrations. The baseball blue-bloods, as usual, thought we were being lowbrow and making a sham of their game.

Soon everyone was shooting off post-game fireworks, but that's not the only legacy of our cheap theatrics.

One night I was admiring the fireworks going off high above Comiskey Park when I noticed the reflection of the colors against the glass of an empty press box that once had been used during games of the Chicago Cardinals football team.

As usual, we were a little short on cash. We wanted to re-sign Chet Lemon, who at the time was one of baseball's better outfielders, and needed to generate about $70,000. We came up with the idea of renting the empty press box to groups that wanted their own private seating area. We threw in beer and a rib dinner.

In the Houston Astrodome, they had an "owner's box" where the Big Kahuna entertained family and friends. I called our seating area a "skybox" and it was immediately successful, even though the box had no bathroom and was accessible only via a catwalk. Within 3 days of its introduction, it had sold out for the season.

Now, had I known that over the next two decades, the luxury box concept was going to result in the rampant escalation of ticket prices and make sports less accessible for families and middle-class fans as teams increasingly catered to corporations and wealthy customers, I might have had some second thoughts about my skybox. I'm not especially proud of the fact that dozens of perfectly good stadiums and arenas were torn down and replaced almost solely at taxpayer expense largely because they lacked sufficient luxury box seating. I'm downright ashamed that I unwittingly helped inspire the $295 club seat tickets now commonplace in the NFL, to say nothing of the $100 to $200 private club tickets in baseball, hockey, and basketball.

Forget Disco Demolition; this is my true cardinal sin. For my penance, I have spent the latter part of my career creating fun, affordable, family-oriented evenings of minor league baseball. I hope society can forgive me for opening Pandora's skybox.

I use the skybox, however, to illustrate the power of maintaining that childlike curiosity. People like Dad have such strong personalities that they can mobilize and motivate people; Dad could transfer that "why not?" vision to others.

If you approach things with optimism and with the mentality that any obstacle can be overcome with good humor, preparation, brainpower, and a little bit of luck, nothing is outside the realm of possibility.

I likely never would have considered the skybox idea were it not for this attitude Dad inspired. Look at any wonderful idea that's ever transpired, and chances are it came about, like the skybox, without a logical set of circumstances.

But if you glance underneath the surface, you'll find that it was in response to someone asking the simple question of "why not?"—a product of maintaining that childlike curiosity.

Lesson 6: Money Has Little Relationship to Enjoying Life

There were brief periods in Dad's life when he was considered wealthy, but he couldn't get rid of money fast enough. Dad was generous to a fault. Give him a pile of cash, and he'd immediately look for ways to get rid of it. In our Catholic household, money was a more taboo subject than sex.

Hank Greenberg, Dad's close friend and the great Detroit Tigers slugger, became a shrewd investor after his playing career. He begged Dad to invest in the stock market—and later mentioned that if Dad had invested $50,000 with him, it would have been worth $3 million. Hank would shake his head and marvel that Dad would spend more time talking with a cab driver than about the stock market.

Dad didn't care. In 1981, when he sold the White Sox, he and Mom burned personal IOUs in the amount of $250,000. Dad never asked for IOUs, but people insisted on scribbling down amounts on pieces of paper. My parents took the stack of scraps, opened a bottle of champagne, and lit a match.

Dad was uncomfortable with wealth and dynasties. He didn't like nepotism, even though he was both the giver and recipient of it. As Mom famously said, "Bill started on the right side of the tracks and spent his whole life trying to get over to the other side."

Other baseball owners were elitists, and that concept repulsed him. He preferred the people in the stands, believing that the price of the seat was inversely proportional to the knowledge and quality of the fan.

Many people define themselves by their net worth. If they lose the fortune, they feel there's no way to regain it. Dad was flush each time he sold a ball club, but there always were debts to be paid and a large family to feed and school. The IRS always seemed to be calling.

The only wealth he believed he had was a great working knowledge of the English language and of literature, a skill honed through thousands of hours spent reading. Armed with that knowledge, he had the means to accomplish whatever he wanted.

Don't spend so much time in the pursuit of money. Pursue knowledge from books and people instead.

I loved the fact that Dad never preached. If you asked, he'd explain what he was doing. If you had a better idea, he'd welcome an argument. He achieved legendary status as an innovator but never presumed he had all the answers. In fact, he constantly turned to others for answers and had a genuine curiosity about everything.

Dad reveled in conversation; he'd be disappointed at how when you walk into most bars today, the music is cranked so loud it's impossible to speak to anyone. It no doubt would frustrate him how our culture has become so self-absorbed.

Most of us spend our lives chasing fame and fortune. Dad obtained the former and sometimes the latter. But neither was the reason he enjoyed life to the degree most people can only dream about.

Lesson 7: Be Color-Blind, Gender-Blind, Age-Blind, and Experience-Blind

Dad loved to argue about prejudice. He loved to challenge people to justify it from an intellectual standpoint. Nobody ever could offer an explanation beyond "that's the way it is."

Dad was color-blind—and the least judgmental person I ever met. Five years before Jackie Robinson broke baseball's color barrier, Dad had planned to purchase the Philadelphia Phillies and stock the team with stars from the Negro League. Unfortunately, the other owners and baseball commissioner Kenesaw Mountain Landis rejected the idea.

Dad eventually integrated the American League by signing Larry Doby in 1947 to play for the Cleveland Indians, 3 months after Robinson became the first black player in the National League.

Larry lost his dad when he was 8 years old and came to regard Bill Veeck as a second father.

"He didn't see color," Doby told the *New York Times* in 1997. "To me, he was, in every sense, color-blind. And I always knew he was there for me. He always seemed to know when things were bad, if things were getting to me. He'd call up and say, 'Let's go out, let's get something to eat.'"

Dad stood behind Larry. When he was introduced to his Indians teammates, several refused to shake his hand.

"The next year Bill Veeck eliminated about five of the guys who were discourteous to me," Doby told Art Rust Jr., author of *Get That Nigger Off the Field: An Oral History of Black Ballplayers from the Negro Leagues to the Present Man in Baseball.*

In 1978, Dad hired Larry to replace Bob Lemon as manager for the final four months of the season, making Larry only the second black to be a major league manager.

When we moved to Easton, Maryland, the Avalon movie theater still was segregated. Dad solved that by having first-run movies flown in and staging movie night in an outbuilding on our property. Everyone was invited.

When Civil Rights leader Gloria Richardson led a movement to dismantle segregation in nearby Cambridge, Maryland, the settlement between her group and the Maryland National Guard was negotiated on our porch.

My parents never had to preach equality. It was obvious by the way they lived their lives.

Dad used to tell the story about how his father, Chicago Cubs president William Veeck Sr., once took him into the box office after a game and dumped all the cash on the table.

"What color is the money?" William Sr. asked.

"Green."

"What color are the people who put that money in your till?"

"I don't know," Dad said.

"Precisely."

Dad never viewed anyone as inferior, and that propelled his business. He spoke, ate, and drank with everybody. A bricklayer could relate to Bill Veeck because he had a few beers with him and Dad took a genuine interest in him. Fans stumbled over each other at the ballpark to sit and watch a few innings with him because he made people feel good. They bought tickets not just because they were baseball fans but because they wanted to support their good buddy, Bill.

I'm convinced Dad met and knew more people than anyone who ever lived. He once took me to see Louis Armstrong perform, and before the concert, Satchmo leaned over and said, "Bill, how you doin'?"

I have no idea how Dad knew Louis Armstrong, but this kind of stuff happened all the time. It wasn't just celebrities. In 1963, he and I went to Washington and stood in line for 16 hours in bitter cold to walk past President Kennedy's casket. As we made our way to the back of the line, dozens of people said hello. These weren't just people who recognized Dad; many knew him from having a beer with him or watching baseball with him.

Some of them offered us a chance to cut in line. Heck, Dad could have pulled some strings and gotten us up there without waiting. But that wasn't him.

Dad didn't preach equality; he wore it on his sleeve. The reason people lined up to work for him was that he fostered this atmosphere that we're all in this together. Even though he was the owner/president, there was this one-for-all mentality. He'd correct people who said "I love working for you."

"*With* you," he'd say. "I work with you. You work with me."

Dad always insisted people call him Bill, never Mr. Veeck. That created a relaxed atmosphere at his ballpark, but it didn't mean employees viewed him with any less respect.

On the contrary, he commanded great respect because that's how he treated everyone—regardless of age, color, gender, or experience.

Lesson 8: A Terrible Thing Happens When You Don't Hustle–Nothing

In our house, being a hustler was and is a very positive thing. To be a hustler is to scuffle, work hard, and improve your circumstances. To hustle is to convince someone that something is blue even when it appears to be red. Of Dad's three books, *The Hustler's Handbook* is my favorite because it captures the essence of his business philosophy.

Dad reveled in the notion of hustling something for nothing. Even when he had the money to pay for it, he'd rather hustle it. He felt it makes you more creative and keeps you on edge.

Companies can create valuable publicity for free, but they'd rather pay dearly for it in the form of advertising and marketing. Why pay for something when you can get it for free if you just hustle a little? Come up with a reason for the media to write about you. If nothing else, trade some of your product to radio and television outlets for some of theirs.

A hustler is someone who scoffs at the indentured servitude of corporate America and decides to make it on her own by being an entrepreneur or independent contractor, or otherwise creatively piecing together a living. You can hustle within the corporate framework—and enjoy it if it's a Fun Is Good environment—but there isn't a successful entrepreneur who hasn't hustled.

In the early stages of a business, you have to hustle to survive. You'll work 24/7 and do absolutely everything to make it work. Even after you've achieved the money and success, you look back fondly on the time when you had to hustle. That's why you see so many successful entrepreneurs build second and third businesses.

Dad got that—it's why he did five stints as a baseball owner. The joy was in the journey, not in reveling in the success. Everyone looks proudly at something they built not just because it's successful but because it was created from scratch.

We reminisce about those tough times because that's when we were most creative and resourceful.

It's like that Jimmy Buffett song "Peanut Butter Conspiracy," where he sings about the guy who occasionally shoplifts food long after he becomes successful just so he doesn't lose his touch in case he falls on hard times again.

Hustling is closely linked with ambition, which for some reason carries a negative connotation in this country. Ambition is good. It's only when it's linked to greed, corruption, and stepping on other people that it's a bad thing.

Ambition, like hustling, means you're going to better yourself and do something positive for your family. Where would we be without ambition and hustling? Think of the people who do the same job year after year, never advancing, taking a chance, or doing anything different. What a sad, monotonous way to go through life.

I marvel at how 9-to-5 people scoff at self-employed professionals who earn a living by hustling. Their income is determined not by a fixed salary but by how much they hustle. The upside is tremendous; the security, ironically, is greater. If you have 17 gigs or clients, it's not the end of the world when you lose 2 or 3. Chances are you have a couple of new ones to replace them. But someone with one full-time job often is devastated, at least temporarily, when he becomes unemployed.

At the corporate level, many executives think hustling is beneath them, or they don't know how to pull it off. They'd rather just pay millions in advertising and marketing.

The basic concept is to get someone else to pay for something you thought of that will benefit him. If it's a good enough idea, the person paying for it gets more out of it than the creator. The exploding scoreboard generated a great deal of exposure for Union 76, especially when it was pictured on the cover of *Sports Illustrated*.

If you own an insurance business, can you offer your services for free in exchange for advertising? Bartering is a form of hustling. Can you come up with a wacky radio campaign or contest? (We'll get into this more in Chapter 7.)

Some people who are good hustlers pull back the reins once they become successful. They want to get away from that 20-hour-a-day lifestyle, even though they know they had more fun that way. If you can pay for it, why bother hustling? Who wants to go back to the way it was?

That goes against everything Bill Veeck represented. Hustling new ideas and reinventing yourself is what keeps life fun. Major League Baseball often looks down upon minor league baseball hustling and its promotions, calling them bush league, only to adopt some of them later.

Major League Baseball officials keep expecting the game to sell itself. Dad used to marvel at how his fellow owners thought hustling was beneath them. No other business operates this way. Baseball owners continue to take their business, with its graying fan base and declining popularity, for granted.

Many companies have no idea how to be creative. These are the people who never have had to meet payroll themselves. When you've had to come up with money yourself, suddenly hustling doesn't look so bad.

What do you have to lose by hustling? Absolutely nothing.

30 Tons a Day

I went to work for Dad at the Suffolk Downs horse track near Boston during my first summer in college. At first, I worked in the betting windows, until someone cracked down and told Dad he couldn't let his son take bets (I wasn't 21).

Dad assigned me the job of "paddock manager," and I was excited about what sounded like a prestigious position until I learned the first day that my main duty was to shovel horse manure at the approximate—perhaps slightly exaggerated—rate of 30 tons a day.

I've never forgotten this lesson. I had a gravy job that didn't work out, and Dad had to put me somewhere. Some people are so preoccupied with titles that they'll accept anything if it looks good on a business card.

More important, Dad taught me that even the president's son is not above shoveling manure. We're all in this together, as we discussed in Chapter 3, and everyone should be willing to pitch in—or dig in—wherever needed.

This episode showed me once and for all what a brilliant hustler Bill Veeck was. If he could hustle his own kid, who after 20 years presumably knew all his tricks, imagine how he must have hustled people who never suspected a thing.

Dad's tenure as a racetrack owner is overshadowed by his baseball experience—and that's a shame because it's so illustrative of the value of hustling. In 1969, at the age of 54, he reinvented himself and learned an entirely new business. He immersed himself in horseracing, read everything he could to bring himself up to speed, and brought customer service and creative promotions to an industry known for neither.

Talk about hustling. He successfully sued the state of Massachusetts to allow kids to attend horse races because his customer base was aging and he wanted kids to enjoy these magnificent creatures. Suffolk Downs was kept impeccably clean—its paint job seemed to sparkle from miles away—and it served as the site of one of the most memorable races ever.

Dad staged the "Yankee Gold Club," a grass race luring top horses and jockeys from around the world. Unfortunately, it was one of the hottest days in Boston history, and attendance was disappointing. I have no idea how much money he lost that day, but he must have lost his shirt.

Yet it didn't bother Dad at all, in part because the race received media coverage all over the world. Dad and I drank a lot of beer that night. There were few times I questioned his promotions, but I asked how he could justify the loss.

He just smiled. "McGill, sometimes you just have to take a shot."

Admittedly, we had some other struggles. Like the time we set off fireworks, scaring the horses. That didn't hold us back; we found some pyrotechnics that made little noise but still produced dazzling colors.

Suffolk Downs never was more profitable than when Dad operated it. He took the gig because he needed the money and was scuffling for his family. In many respects, it was his greatest hustle. He ran a dazzling operation, working the town like crazy by speaking three or four times a day. As usual, he was color-blind, gender-blind, and ethnicity-blind with his workforce. He hired people to put 110 percent into their jobs because that's what he gave, and at the end of the day they'd kick back and have beers together.

Veteran horseracing people would sit with Dad and marvel how much this newcomer knew about their business. Even now, that industry invites me to speak at their conventions.

If you hustle, you can become an expert and be successful at anything—at any age.

I took those experiences from Suffolk Downs and applied them when I ran the marketing for a jai alai fronton more than a decade later. Dad dedicated his third book, *30 Ton A Day*, to me in honor of my yeoman efforts as paddock manager.

It was an honor to be so hustled.

· ·

Lesson 9:
Speak to Everyone, Including the Media

Dad built his business largely by speaking to everyone, especially the members of the press. He gave hundreds of speeches a year, and rarely did a day go by when he did not talk to a reporter.

It wasn't just that Dad didn't have money for marketing and advertising; he genuinely enjoyed meeting new people and presenting his message to audiences, along with engaging in give-and-take with the media.

Never miss an opportunity to speak in front of a group. It doesn't matter if it's an audience of 2 or 2,000. There's no easier way to promote a business. Not only that, there's usually free food involved.

You might argue that if you had the last name Veeck and owned a few baseball teams, you'd be a popular keynote speaker. There is some truth to that. But anyone can become a speaker.

Do you belong to a local chamber of commerce? If not, you should. It's a fabulous networking opportunity. Chambers are always looking for speakers. So too are church, fraternal, civic, and charitable organizations. You probably belong to a few already. Never turn down a chance to speak to a trade group.

Some people hate being self-promotional. They find it egotistical or boastful. The truth is it's tough to be successful without a little self-promotion. If you don't toot your own horn, no one else will.

Remember what happens when you don't hustle?

Volunteer to speak. If someone in your office can call around and book you to speak, that's even better. In fact, it's more effective to have someone else call on your behalf. It makes it seem as if you do this so often, you need someone to handle the bookings. (It also makes rejection easier for you to take.)

You might think your story is too boring. "I work in insurance or banking. I can't possibly have anything people would want to listen to."

Every person and every company has a story. I've proven this theory on airplanes all the time. If I talk to the passenger next to me long enough, I'll learn something fascinating about him or her. That unassuming guy in a wheelchair might turn out to be a singer-songwriter and one of Bob Dylan's closest friends. You never know.

When you tell your tale or your company's story, that helps your business, especially once you put some Fun Is Good into it. People will want to be a part of what you're doing, and it will boost the bottom line.

You might think this is irrelevant if you're not an owner of the company. "That's not my job. I never have to worry about speaking in front of groups."

That might be true. But it's hard to think of a skill more valuable than public speaking. At some point in your career, your advancement is going to depend on how well you can communicate your ideas to an audience. That's especially true if you run the business or ultimately start your own.

Don't worry if you're not an effective speaker initially. Dad wasn't either. Heck, there were some that believed he never was that good, at least by conventional standards. Someone from the esteemed Brookings Institution attended one of Dad's speeches and graded him on a standardized 20-point scale. Dad failed every point and was given further deductions for smoking and holding a bottle of beer on stage.

The report concluded that Dad did nothing by the book—but should not change a thing because the crowd loved him. That's all that counts.

It's easy to develop public speaking skills. Read everything you can. Keep a dictionary and thesaurus on your desk. Join a Toastmasters club. Attend seminars and listen to how people speak. Borrow phrases, especially self-deprecating ones. Instead of zoning out in meetings, study people who have the power to captivate an audience.

If you become a decent speaker, you will find it easy to deal with the press. No group gets a worse rap than the media. It's true that journalists can misquote, misinterpret, and generally make your life miserable, sometimes unintentionally. But that's no reason to dismiss the entire group and assume that the press is the enemy.

Too many companies take the wrong approach when it comes to media relations. They go on the defensive, providing as little information as they can and making it as difficult as possible for media outlets to tell their story. The bunker mentality takes over.

Many companies have "crisis management" people whose job descriptions entail dealing with the media in times of scandal. That makes sense, though even then I would suggest there are more forthright methods of dealing with a negative media spotlight. The problem is that companies treat the media as if they're in permanent crisis mode.

Companies think nothing of spending millions on advertising and marketing but miss a wonderful opportunity to get the same exposure for free. If your story can be told through print or television, you'll get priceless publicity that's more credible because it wasn't paid for; it's objective.

You can't beat that deal. Yet most executives cringe at the thought of dealing with the press. They'd rather hire spokespeople who at best provide the media with vanilla comments and at worst make it impossible for reporters to do a story on your company.

When you work in minor league baseball, you don't have the luxury of huge marketing and advertising budgets, so you do whatever you can to generate publicity. This isn't easy, not with 30 big-league teams drawing more attention, to say nothing of hundreds of other minor league teams. News outlets are not going to cover your games, so you must come up with other reasons for them to pay attention.

Any company can generate publicity. If your business is even moderately successful, there's no doubt a remarkable tale about how the company got off the ground. Are you doing something cutting edge? If so, let the media know.

Still skeptical? Dad once held a press conference to announce that he would be expanding the ladies' restrooms at Comiskey Park. This was in the mid-1970s, when Miller introduced Lite beer and women started drinking more suds. Given Dad's reputation, the press was likely to show up for any announcement, but it still illustrates how little it takes to draw media coverage.

If a tree falls in the woods and no one is around to hear it, as the saying goes, does it make a sound? I'm not sure, but I do know if you don't toot your own horn a little, you can't assume the media is going to hear the message.

Dad recognized that dealing with the media was a two-way street. He could provide information and access, and the reporters in turn let him know what was going on throughout the league. The same is true in any business. You can glean insight about your competition from media sources.

Few companies take advantage of this. They look at the media as the enemy. Dad made it simple when dealing with the media. He did not talk off the record, and if he didn't know something, he'd admit it and promise to get an answer.

Admittedly, most of Dad's career transpired in the pre-Watergate era, long before Bob Woodward and Carl Bernstein redefined journalism. But unless you've done something wrong, there's no reason to view the media as the enemy.

More often than not, the media approach you to report on something you probably want publicized. Why wouldn't you drop everything to help them help you?

Reporters can become the enemy if you constantly lie, mislead and attempt to spin them. They'll tune you out if you inundate them with meaningless press releases.

But if you learn to speak and deal effectively with the media, your business will grow exponentially.

Lesson 10: Live a Life of Creativity

Dad was the most knowledgeable man I've ever met, and it was all because of reading. He read everything from Elmore Leonard to mainstream literature to Herman Melville's *Omoo* and *Typee* to books on engineering.

If Dad was interested in something, he'd buy a dozen books on the subject, devour them, learn everything he could, and then go out and apply his new expertise. He raised orchids and tropical fish, created elaborate mobiles to hang from the ceiling, and enjoyed woodworking. He loved word games and charades. He had a green thumb when it came to shrubs and flowers. He planted ivy on the outfield walls of Wrigley Field, perhaps the most famous signature touch of any sports venue of all time.

Dad always encouraged me to read the entire paper. There's nothing wrong with focusing on the sports section, he'd say, especially when that's your business, but you need to read every section because your customers do, and ideas will come from everywhere.

A life of creativity involves taking risks, whether it's staging the Yankee Cup, hiring a midget pinch-hitter, or something more important like signing Larry Doby. It involves asking "Why not?" every single day and proving the skeptics wrong by continually trying the impossible. It involves seeing the potential in exploding scoreboards, square beer cans, and ivy-covered walls.

A life of creativity involves bringing out the creativity in others and seeking their opinions. It involves lots of laughter, never taking yourself too seriously, and dealing with adversity with a smile. It involves reinventing yourself at 54, seeking out speaking opportunities, and never missing the opportunity to learn about someone.

Dad has been dead nearly two decades, and his lessons seem more appropriate now in a world where we've sucked much of the joy out of the workplace and evolved into a culture where few know how to laugh and have fun.

If we learn nothing else from Bill Veeck, let's remember that it's possible to be the hardest-working person and still be the one who has the most fun.

FUN IS GOOD

Chapter 5 Summary and Exercises (Lessons from Dad)

- Answer your own phone. You never know who might call.
- Spend less time talking about yourself and more time asking others about themselves.
- A clean environment makes for a strong first impression.
- The size of your bank account does not dictate how much you will enjoy life.
- Laugh at adversity.
- Never lose your childhood curiosity. Always ask "Why not?"
- List the last five books you've read. How many were for fun? Are you reading enough?
- Be a hustler.
- Never miss an opportunity to speak in front of a group. Public speaking is a valuable skill. List three places you could speak in the coming months.
- It's never too late to reinvent yourself.

Chapter 6

The Power of Irreverence

I am often accused of engaging in cheap theatrics. I happily plead guilty. I love fireworks and blowing things up. I never miss a chance to poke good-natured fun at a worthy target to promote my business and create laughter. No ridiculous anniversary should go uncelebrated. If it involves rock 'n' roll, all the better.

Some big-time CEOs look at our silly promotions and shameless attempts to generate exposure and think that their Fortune 500 companies are somehow above all of that. That's simply not true. You do a disservice to your business if you don't engage in some occasional cheap theatrics.

Let's say you make widgets. Let the assembly line run until you have 10,000 of them piled up, and then call the press. It makes a great visual. Celebrate your 1 millionth widget produced. If you do such things, then your stuffy company suddenly is seen as having a sense of humor. It's good for business.

When it comes to irreverence, it's tough to beat the folks at Hormel Foods Corporation and their marketing of SPAM. No one will admit that they have SPAM in their home, let alone eat it. God only knows what's in SPAM. Canned meat? No way, not for me.

But SPAM has a full line of popular licensed merchandise. There's a SPAM fan club and a SPAM-mobile that travels the country promoting SPAM. SPAM sometimes sponsors the Zambonis that clean the ice at hockey games, turning the vehicles into "SPAM-bonis."

SPAM gets Fun Is Good. Somebody at SPAM early on figured that they needed to take this self-deprecating approach because canned meat in and of itself wasn't going to cut it. Realizing that people made fun of the product, they used it as their marketing campaign. Now SPAM is one of those things—it's so uncool, it's cool.

There's even a SPAM museum in Austin, Minnesota, on the corner of Main Street and SPAM Boulevard. Billed as "16,500 square feet of SPAM Nirvana," it's housed in a handsome brick building on the site of a former Kmart. Outside there's a life-size bronze statue of a farmer taking two hogs to market. Billboards in the area tout "The SPAM Museum: Believe the Hype."

Inside, you're greeted by a "SPAMbassador." There's a 3,500-can "Wall of SPAM," a SPAM theater, and even an interactive "SPAM Exam." The SPAM gift shop has a full line of merchandise, including SPAM watches, T-shirts, golf bags, and bumper stickers.

Even the SPAM name has a great story behind it. Some believe SPAM is short for "spiced ham" or "shoulder of pork and ham." Others believe it came about as part of a wild New Year's Eve celebration where Jay Hormel, son of the father, offered a free drink for each naming contest entry.

SPAM is the cornerstone of Hormel's $4 billion annual empire, which includes brands such as Dinty Moore and Jennie-O. SPAM has been around since 1937, and there's no way it would have survived for so long if its employees didn't have some fun with it. If you think it's impossible to put a little Fun Is Good into your product, company, or career, consider SPAM. If the people can create a culture of fun out of canned meat, then anything is possible.

It's not just SPAM. Many companies pay advertising agencies millions of dollars to craft ad campaigns that portray the company and its products as hip, edgy, and irreverent. Isn't that what modern advertising is all about?

If you have the budget, go right ahead and hire the professionals to do Fun Is Good for you. If you'd like to save some money, have fun, and flex your creative muscles, then try and foster that Fun Is Good mentality in the office.

Most of my so-called brilliant ideas have come from employees, all of whom feel empowered to suggest anything they feel could help our company, no matter how outlandish it might seem.

Irreverence is vital not just to marketing and promotion but also in creating a productive office culture. People get the wrong idea about irreverence. It's not just about playing practical jokes on colleagues or holding Hawaiian shirt day. It's about creating an environment in which people take their jobs, but not themselves, seriously.

Creating irreverence in a company is an ongoing process. It's usually easier if you do cutting-edge work. Technology companies can be that way, though you might also get an *Office Space* environment. Ad agencies have an inherent irreverence because of the mix of writers and artists. Humor flows naturally. In that kind of environment, it's easy to stop in the middle of the day and have a game of Nerf basketball, with bodies flying into walls and doors.

It was Yossarian, the protagonist in my favorite book, Joseph Heller's *Catch-22,* who said that if everyone else was acting crazy, he'd be crazy to act otherwise. (I knew I'd get some mileage out of my college thesis!) Irreverence in the office is contagious.

It's the juxtaposition of the serious workplace and the leisure-time mentality. It's marrying those so there's a balance. It's not that you don't take your work seriously, but you need to relieve the pressure. After all, what is creativity but the pressure to constantly top your previous idea with something even more brilliant? You need those quick releases in the office. Instead of exploding, you want to redirect that anger and frustration.

Where do you begin, especially if you have a high-starch corporate office? You have to find a soul mate, a person who can be your partner in crime. There's always somebody. Admittedly, you have to pick your targets, but if you get to know people, you can read them pretty quickly.

Busting on one another in the workplace keeps things loose. It's like the WD-40 of life. You can poke fun at anything except politics, religion, race, and mothers. Everything else is pretty much fair game. It's not mean-spirited, but it does have an edge to it. Remember, there's no easier way to deliver a message than by making people laugh.

When I broke my leg, the one-legged Veeck jokes were relentless. Each of our clubs issued press releases about my trip to the disabled list. This meant as much as the food, flowers, and gifts I received.

It's not as difficult as you might think. Everyone wants to have some fun. The problem is they don't know how to do it. You have to prove to them that it's okay. Even the stuffiest, most serious bosses can be brought around to our side.

Prior to the 1999 baseball season, I was hired by Vince Naimoli as the senior vice president of marketing for the Tampa Bay Devil Rays. Vince, for all of his success in other businesses, had developed a reputation for having an explosive temper, little patience, and a take-no-prisoners approach to operating a ball club.

Vince also recognized that something was missing from the Devil Rays. For all of the hoopla surrounding the first year of baseball in Tampa Bay, the 1998 season was a disappointment. The team was lousy, as all expansion teams are, but attendance fell short of projections and there wasn't a whole lot of fun at the ballpark.

For all of his bluster, Vince Naimoli has a sense of humor, and I recognized that even he could be the target of my office irreverence.

Vince did not like the idea of selling partial season ticket packages. He felt there was enough excitement surrounding baseball in Tampa Bay to inspire people to purchase full-season ticket packages and attend 81 games a season.

Maybe that was true for 1998, but that no longer was the case after a disappointing season.

For 1999, I introduced the Rays' first-ever partial season ticket packages with a campaign called "Vinnie Goes Mini."

Rays employees said Vince would never go for it. No way would the hard-charging, by-the-corporate-book Vince Naimoli allow himself to be the butt of a joke. But Vince went along, and the campaign worked. It softened his image in the business community, and we sold a lot of mini-plans. Ultimately, my work implementing Fun Is Good with the Devil Rays failed, but it demonstrated that it's possible to poke fun at anyone with the right approach. (We still use the Rays-inspired "Off the Wall" marketing slogan with our Charleston team.)

Irreverence draws attention. A few years ago, Morley Safer came to St. Paul to do a feature on the Saints for *60 Minutes*. At one point, he was interviewing me in the concourse and I began to feel a little nervous. He kept looking at a sign over the exit.

"That's really terrible," he said finally.

"You've been looking at that sign for 45 seconds," I said. "That's what they call an impression in advertising."

"But doesn't it bother you that it's kind of tasteless?"

"No, it really doesn't," I said.

The sign is for a local funeral home. Its slogan: "Drive carefully. We can wait."

In Charleston, an attorney who specializes in DWI (driving while intoxicated) cases is one of our sponsors. His name and contact information is printed on each souvenir cup. We encourage people to drink responsibly, and we cut beer sales off long before the game ends. But if fans find themselves in trouble with the law, they need only turn to the source of the problem for help.

Irreverence sells. I don't know at what point we all got so uptight and began to take ourselves too seriously. We're allowed to laugh.

Irreverence goes hand in hand with creativity. I was speaking to a group one day before the Devil Rays kicked off the 1999 season and a reporter raised his hand. "Hey," he said. "You're always doing stupid things. Let's see you do something stupid."

At first, I was a little taken aback. I mean, even I have feelings. But I thought about it for a minute. I looked down at the microphone. It was held together with duct tape. A cord ran down the podium and across the floor and it too was covered with duct tape so that no one would trip over it.

"Isn't duct tape the most marvelous invention?" I said finally. "I think we'll have a Salute to Duct Tape night."

The reporter loved it. "Now that's really stupid!" he said.

The next day, the proposed "Salute to Duct Tape" night was mentioned on the news wire and was picked up by the *Cleveland Plain Dealer.* Not long after I got back to Florida, I got a call from a guy from Manco Inc.

"I want to talk to you about that promotion you were talking about in the *Plain Dealer.*"

I drew a blank. "Pardon me, sir?"

"You know, your Salute to Duct Tape promotion. We're one of the largest manufacturers of duct tape. We call our product 'Duck Tape.'"

"Of course!" I exclaimed. "The Salute to Duck Tape promotion." Then I shuffled some papers and slammed a desk drawer. "I've got that outline right here."

"I have a check here for you . . ."

"Hey, it's 10 percent off if it's cash," I said, borrowing one of Dad's favorite lines.

Now, if you don't think irreverence sells, the Manco executive flew on a Saturday from Cleveland with a sizable check to sponsor the first-ever Salute to Duck Tape night.

The point is this: No idea is too ridiculous or outrageous to consider. That idea came literally out of thin air, but it could just as easily have come from any employee. And if you're not running your business where every employee feels free to contribute an idea to service your clients better, then you should rethink how you run your business.

Be outrageous. It sells, and it's fun. One of the outlandish ideas I'm most proud of is "Mime-O-Vision." I decided that, for one game in St. Paul, where we did not have instant replay capability on the scoreboard at the time, we would have five mimes stand on the dugout and reenact close plays.

The fans hated it. The crowd of 6,300 fans started throwing hot dogs in record numbers. They were buying the hot dogs and not even unwrapping them, just throwing them at the mimes. We were sending concession workers out to the supermarket to buy more franks and buns.

By the fifth inning, the mimes were hunkered down, trying their best to dodge the hot dogs. By the sixth inning, they were very upset. By the seventh, they were saying things that weren't very mime-like.

We sold thousands of hot dogs that night and had the highest-grossing night in the history of the St. Paul Saints. The promotion—this outrageous promotion—was a roaring success.

The next morning, the headline of the *Minneapolis Star Tribune* read something along the lines of "Promotion Fails," alongside a color photo of a mime being pelted with hot dogs. This ran across the front page. Not the front page of the sports section, the front page of the entire paper. Do you know what that did for my business? You can't buy that kind of publicity at any price. In the sports section, there was another story on how the promotion had bombed. All told, the paper devoted more than 40 column inches to how dumb this promotion was. Somehow, the editors and reporters missed the irony.

And yet, all over the Twin Cities, the fourteenth-largest media market in the country, people were laughing. Remember, people need to laugh. The media might have hated Mime-O-Vision, but the customers loved it. And theirs is the only opinion that counts.

You don't need a ballpark to try things like Mime-O-Vision. Years ago, people would win shopping sprees where they had 90 seconds to grab whatever they could. Pizzerias would award a year's worth of pizza to the winner of a pie-eating contest. My dad used to say that it's barely noteworthy to give one bottle of beer to each of a thousand fans, but it's a big deal to give a thousand bottles of beer to one lucky winner.

Do those things cost money? Of course, but the return on investment in the form of publicity and customer goodwill is enormous. Not only that, but it injects Fun Is Good into your company, and people want to associate themselves with you.

You can't overestimate the power of irreverence. Look at a company like Pier 1 Imports. When it was founded in 1962, it sold beads, incense, and other funky stuff. You never would have figured this company to have staying power. Granted, it overhauled its product line and moved stores from malls to stand-alone locations, but just as important were the ad campaigns that portrayed it as an off-the-wall, irreverent company.

A few years ago, former *Cheers* actress Kirstie Alley starred in a series of whimsical commercials for Pier 1. She didn't wink at the camera, but her expression was one of someone sharing an inside joke. You weren't sure what the joke was, but you left with an impression of Pier 1 as an off-the-wall company.

Ditto for RadioShack. It started in 1921 as a store for ham radio operators and electronics buffs. Even as recently as the early 1990s, it tended to attract the types of geeky people who took radios apart for kicks. Did anyone other than sportswriters use RadioShack's primitive Tandy computers?

Nobody would admit to going to RadioShack. God only knew who shopped there. Probably the same people who ate SPAM or bought Chia Pets.

Then a funny thing happened. RadioShack paired actress Teri Hatcher and football great Howie Long together for a series of whimsical commercials that coincided with the reinvention of the company. Now the company sold cell phones, high-end electronics, and things people actually used.

Its marketing slogan—"You've Got Questions, We've Got Answers"—paid tribute to its radio geek days. The difference was RadioShack made it cool to be clueless about technology. They borrowed a page from the publishers of the *For Dummies* books. They made it not only acceptable but hip to admit a lack of knowledge.

Like SPAM, RadioShack positioned itself as being so uncool it was cool.

Are RadioShack and Pier 1 run with a Fun Is Good mentality, or do they just have advertising agencies that understand the value of irreverence? I'm not sure, but I do know that a company does not have to pay millions to an agency in order to become irreverent. If they're miserable places to work, they've succeeded only in becoming irreverent externally.

It doesn't take much to loosen up an office. Sports teams understand that "locker room chemistry" is just as important as talent and work ethic. Good teams usually have a couple of people who keep the clubhouse loose with jokes, pranks, and an attitude that keeps colleagues from taking themselves too seriously.

That's even more crucial in an office setting. Retired athletes always reminisce about the clubhouse and the good-natured ribbing that went on there. Think back to a job you really enjoyed. It probably wasn't the position or the money as much as it was a freewheeling atmosphere where nothing was off limits.

It's lucrative to be the person who keeps things loose. Many an athlete has hung on for a couple of extra years, long after his talent warranted it, because of the intangible he brought to his workplace. In the corporate world, that ability is perhaps even more valuable. It can make up for a lack of book smarts or natural talent.

Where do you find these people? That's easy: Look at résumés differently. Search for off-the-wall hobbies and experiences. Do these people have easygoing personalities? Do they make you laugh in the interview? How do they interact with people they meet?

We've hired people from local comedy clubs. After all, most of them work at night for peanuts and could use a day job. Occasionally we lose one of them to the national comedy circuit—some of them do make it big—but more often we discover someone who is ready to give up on the unforgiving world of stand-up and is looking for a fun place to work. One of those ex-comics, Fran Zeuli, is now a successful executive in the cable television industry and a part owner of our Brockton Rox baseball team.

Fostering an irreverent atmosphere can be as simple as installing a dartboard on the wall. It's a nonverbal way of loosening up the office. People tend to be aggressive, and it's tough to walk past a dartboard without stopping to throw a few.

At some point, usually after college, people lose that sense of irreverence, the ability to poke fun at a situation. Why is that? Look at a movie like *The Blues Brothers*. A plot involving guys getting out of jail, violating parole, and putting the band back together is funny because we all like to think we'd act the same way if only we could. The same is true for *Animal House*. Who wouldn't want to live that devil-may-care college life forever?

Everyone has to grow up, but the human condition demands that at some point we rebel a little. How else do you explain the unbridled popularity of Halloween—or our partner Jimmy Buffett? Sure, his music is thought provoking and catchy, but his brilliance is in inspiring hordes of middle-age people to put on Hawaiian shirts and flip-flops in the middle of winter and head out to his shows. Why? Because Buffett connects with the contempt everyone has for the button-down, corporate existence many of us swore we'd never endure. For one night, we're 22 again, living in Key West, without a care in the world.

What's wrong with a work environment that provides a little taste of that? If people are happy and free to speak their minds and wisecrack, they will exceed all expectations for productivity.

Remember in the early 1990s when it became fashionable to have "casual Friday"? How phony was that? Does that mean that for 4 days you're uptight and that on Friday you can wear a pair of jeans and all was forgotten? Even in jeans, you can have a high-starch work environment. Give me a place where I can feel free to be irreverent and poke fun at things, and I'll gladly wear my khakis and tie 5 days a week.

So how do you become irreverent? If you continually expose yourself to magazines, radio, television, and the Internet—which is impossible not to even if you try—you'll find that these ideas come constantly.

This is how we come up with most of our ideas. Like the time we staged "Tonya Harding Mini-Bat Night" in Charleston. This was not long after the 1994 Winter Olympics, when associates of Tonya whacked skating rival Nancy Kerrigan with a tire iron. Tasteless? Perhaps, but we were hardly the last to capitalize on Tonya's notoriety. (Mini-Bat Night was the first time I've ever signed a contract where I promised not to include mentions of "black batons or hubcaps" in the promotion.)

Not long after the Enron scandal, we held Enron Night in Portland, Oregon, where we were consulting for the local minor league team. Fans were greeted at the gates of PGE Park with paper shredders, and attendance figures were continually revised over the next few days, with great fanfare. The big irony, of course, was that Portland General Electric, the title sponsor of the ballpark, was owned by Enron.

We received dozens of letters and e-mails from people wondering how we could make fun of people losing their jobs and retirement savings. We weren't poking fun at them but at the scoundrels running Enron. Those guys deserved all the grief we could give them.

Of course, sometimes you can push the envelope too far. Take the time our Charleston RiverDogs hosted the Savannah Sand Gnats on Friday, April 13, which also happened to be Good Friday. I've always found Savannah fascinating. Between the ghosts, cemeteries, drag queens, and everything else that was perfectly captured in the book *Midnight in the Garden of Good and Evil,* it's a mystical place.

We decided to stage Voodoo Night. The first 500 fans were to receive voodoo dolls—at least until the protests started. We were clobbered in the newspapers. This time, Veeck had gone too far. As with our proposed Vasectomy Night, the Catholic Church weighed in with a big protest.

I thought Voodoo Night was relatively tame compared to some of our other promotions. Unfortunately, it's sometimes difficult to predict the reaction. Bill Murray was in town during this firestorm and recommended that I issue a press release, apologize, and fall on my sword, which I did.

We called off Voodoo Night, and I suppose that's an example of crossing the line from irreverence to poor taste. But I'd rather crash and burn every once in a while than be so timid that nothing innovative is ever attempted.

Maybe your office doesn't have a use for these kinds of promotions, though I'd argue that any business can benefit from this thinking. If nothing else, why not hold a themed party where you poke fun at something in the news?

People just want to laugh, even those who seem to have no sense of humor. I once gave a speech to a group of Honeywell International engineers. The intellectual power of these folks was staggering and I was intimidated. They dealt with concepts I couldn't begin to comprehend. But these seemingly serious people with staggering IQs were the greatest audience I've ever had. What they wanted more than anything was someone to come up and point out that they have foibles. It was a huge release.

Current events provide an endless stream of material. How else would David Letterman and Jay Leno fill five monologues a week? Just take something out of the news and run with it. In 2002, the Major League Baseball All-Star Game ended in a tie for the first time ever. The game, played in Milwaukee, ran into extra innings and when the teams ran out of pitchers, Commissioner Bud Selig ruled it a 7 to 7 stalemate.

The tie was an embarrassment to baseball and especially to Selig, the blind trust owner of the Brewers, who for 3 days had reveled in his role as host in his new publicly funded ballpark.

Instead, fans again were reminded that baseball somehow manages to survive in spite of the people who run it.

Naturally, we watched the event closely, and the next day the St. Paul Saints announced "Tie One on for Bud" night. We promised to give away to select fans neckties emblazoned with a caricature of the commissioner. Tom Whaley, our vice president and team attorney, issued a formal press release, tongue firmly in cheek.

"In addition to suspending our club policy, which restricts the appearance of neckties on the premises, we've petitioned the league to investigate the prospect of having all our games end in tie scores," Whaley announced. "We thereby reduce the risk of anyone getting hurt physically or emotionally by the random vagaries associated with on-field losses or extra innings."

Earlier in the 2002 season, with Major League Baseball bracing for yet another work stoppage, the Saints gave out seat cushions with Selig's image printed on one side and the mug of players' union chief Don Fehr on the other. Fans could express their displeasure by choosing whom to sit on, though it was a tough decision because fans tended to blame both parties. (In a rare display of sanity, the owners and players compromised and narrowly averted a work stoppage for the first time in 30 years.)

The Lords of Baseball never stop providing us fodder, but you can find material everywhere. Celebrities and political figures are nonstop inspirations.

In the summer of 2004, as the nation got ready for the Presidential election, we decided to stage our own straw poll. At each of our six ballparks, along with a seventh park owned by a club that wanted to participate, we put out 500 bobblehead dolls, 250 for each candidate. The first 500 fans could choose a doll and, based on how they selected, we determined the winner. If the supply of one doll vanished with 75 of the other remaining, we counted the vote as 250 to 175. (We still gave out the rest of the losing dolls, though some fans passed on the offer. For the record, President Bush defeated Senator Kerry, four precincts to three.)

With our teams scattered throughout the country, with the exception of the West Coast, we considered it a relatively scientific sampling. With so many polls out there, ours didn't look any less official than some, and we generated plenty of media coverage. We made sure with our team in Fort Myers, Florida, to play up the ballot-counting controversy of the 2000 presidential election.

Any company can benefit from a little impertinence. A few years ago, a clergyman asked me to speak at his church on a Saturday night. The members of the congregation must have felt the apocalypse was upon them when they saw Mike Veeck take the pulpit, but they listened to my speech, which was about the "Church of Baseball," and how at the beginning of every season, hope springs eternal and everyone is optimistic that this will be the year their team wins the championship.

I took questions afterward, and someone noted that while the Saints were playing to sellout crowds every night, how could I be bullish for baseball if attendance in the majors was down?

Now I don't normally defend Major League Baseball, but something about the tone of the questioner's voice set me off. After all, this is the game I love. It didn't help that I was missing a softball game at Midway Stadium pitting the Saints front office against employees from the city of St. Paul. Bill Murray and his brother Brian were in town to play for the Saints, and I was missing a great party.

So I fired right back.

"What about your attendance? You guys play to 65 percent capacity every Sunday even though you have the greatest product in the world. You're selling hope. People can walk away from church every Sunday feeling like winners. I can't guarantee that. Heck, some of my teams rarely can provide a winning experience. But yet your attendance figures are worse than mine."

He was obviously skeptical. "How can I apply what you do here?"

I thought fast. "Let's take the next business quarter—13 weeks. Each week, you give away a trading card of an apostle. At the end of 12 weeks, you have the set. For the 13th week, give out a group shot, the Last Supper perhaps."

The audience was skeptical. No way could they introduce such shameless promotions. This, of course, was long before Mel Gibson marketed his *The Passion of the Christ* movie directly to church groups, with all manner of licensed merchandise.

Weeks earlier, when the clergyman had asked me to speak, he mentioned that the religion writer from the *Minneapolis Star Tribune* would be on hand, along with a photographer. I had forgotten this, not that it mattered.

The morning after my speech, there was a picture of me on the front page of the *Minneapolis Star Tribune*. The photographer had captured me standing behind the pulpit during my diatribe, arms extended to the sides. All that was missing was a cross.

Maybe there's hope for Voodoo and Vasectomy Nights yet.

. . . .

What's in a Name?

My son's name is William "Night Train" Veeck. With the exception of teachers, who refer to him as William, everyone else calls him Night Train or simply Train.

I suppose this is an example of irreverence, but really I just wanted him to have a cool name. I don't have a middle name and because I moved so often as a kid—17 times in 11 years—I was never around anywhere long enough to pick up a nickname like Stinky or Mad-Dog. But I always wanted one.

My first wife, Jo, and I were driving to the Miami Arena to see a Jimmy Buffett concert during her pregnancy when I came up with Night Train. I suppose I was inspired by James Brown's song "Night Train" or by the football hall-of-famer Dick "Night Train" Lane, who seemed to me to have the coolest nickname ever.

My dad never liked being William Louis Veeck Jr. He loved his father but wanted to make his own name, which was challenging working in the same business. As a young adult, Dad changed his name legally to Bill Veeck, though he often referred to himself as "Ole Will."

Dad died 3 months before my son arrived, but the William is for him. I figured with a middle name like "Night Train," my son always would be one of the first kids picked for games, regardless of athletic skills.

You never know what a name will mean for a kid. In 1973, a creative man in California named Ramon thought he'd spell his name backward and make it his son's middle name. The kid ended up adopting it when there were too many Anthonys in his class, and now *Nomar* Garciaparra is a household name.

· ·

Fun Is Good Vignette

Ed Droste,
Cofounder, Hooters Restaurants

"People think it was easy. They look at our 375 Hooters restaurants in 10 countries and figure it was as simple as putting some cute girls in orange nylon shorts, coming up with a catchy name, and opening the doors for business."

If only. Back in 1983, not long after we opened the original Hooters in Clearwater, Florida, my partners were growing impatient with the slow traffic. One afternoon, somewhat desperate, I rented a chicken outfit, walked out on the sidewalk in front of the restaurant, and started flapping my wings.

It was about that time that I noticed part of a sunken boat sticking out along the Courtney Campbell Causeway, which connects Clearwater to Tampa. This bright white boat could be seen by thousands of drivers every day. What a wasted opportunity.

I got a can of orange paint and a brush, swam out to the boat, and painted "Hooters" in huge letters. Talk about free publicity. The local media, which had pretty much ignored us, suddenly wanted to know about this wacky little restaurant.

Thankfully, that got the ball rolling, but we were struggling up until that point. We didn't have an advertising budget. Nobody was going to pay for spots on radio and television. All we had was a restaurant in a bad location—it had failed in previous incarnations as a pizza joint and a muffler shop—and nobody knew what we were.

We knew we had a good product—a carefree, beachlike environment with aspects of the neighborhood bar, and the Hooters girls providing the energy and enthusiasm—but I don't know if we would have survived without humor, a sense of irreverence, and a willingness to take chances.

We loved to poke fun at ourselves. None of the six founders had any restaurant experience. On the flip side of the menus, where other eateries typically pat themselves on the back, we noted that in the early days we were "promptly arrested for impersonating restaurateurs." Our motto became "delightfully tacky, yet unrefined," and we applied it to everything.

When we came up with a Hooters calendar, we put the months out of order. One year we included a generic landscape photo in the centerfold so men could flip to an innocuous photo rather than take it down to hide it from people they didn't want to see it.

The Web site for the original Hooters includes an "in case of boss" button. If you're perusing our site and the boss comes along, you can click over to a page that has articles such as "How Reducing Your Salary Can Improve Company Profitability" and "Why Working Overtime Is Good for You."

We recognized that inspirations for goofy promotions and stunts are everywhere. Just follow current events.

In the early 1990s, our original spokesperson and model Lynne Austin was posted on a billboard in center field at Jack Russell Stadium in Clearwater, the spring training home of the Philadelphia Phillies. The team's catcher, Darren Daulton, met Lynne while she was a ball girl, and they later married.

When Darren signed a $19 million contract extension, we snuck into the stadium and pasted a banner across Lynne's billboard that read "$9.5 million."

The players were in on the joke and roared when Darren came onto the field and saw the sign. Sadly, we turned out to be prophetic; Lynne and Darren later divorced.

Jon Gruden, the head coach of the Tampa Bay Buccaneers, remarked a few years ago that he belonged on a Hooters billboard. After all, he had once spent 2 months working as a cook at one of our Tampa locations. So I made up a billboard rendering with Gruden's face attached to the body of a Hooters girl and presented it to him in front of the team.

The Fun Is Good philosophies have worked for us. Whether it's delivering superior customer service, not taking yourself too seriously, or having fun in the office, it's vital to the success of your company.

Customer service is crucial, especially in the discriminating world of the restaurant business. Among the things Hooters girls learn during training are to place a napkin under every beer and make repeat visits to the table, acknowledging the customer. Those things are subtle, but they make a difference.

Listen to your customer. Our staff encourages interaction, and a lot of the heart and soul of our business comes from the customers. One guy told me that his daughter is fighting leukemia and the only thing that cheers her up after a round of chemotherapy is coming into Hooters and getting her fix of 10 chicken wings. Naturally, we make a big deal over her visits.

We strive to be a good neighbor by getting involved in the community. After all, you can't claim to be a neighborhood restaurant if you're not attuned to the neighborhood. We're not shy about our image. Our community involvement, admittedly, is done partially to buffer an image that might be offensive to some. But over time, that civicmindedness makes us more appealing to the community.

Perhaps it's working. Now, when we open new restaurants, we don't hear nearly the protests we once did. Maybe society has changed, and we're not considered as risqué as we once were.

We recently opened a chain of restaurants called "Pete and Shorty's," joking that it was in response to Hooters' becoming too sophisticated. In the ladies' bathrooms we have a statue of Michelangelo's David with nudity covered by a fig leaf. If a lady peeks under the leaf, it triggers an alarm behind the bar. When she comes out, she's handed a button that reads, "I peeked at Pete and Shorty's."

These days, our original ownership group maintains the stores in Tampa Bay, Chicago, and New York City, along with the calendar and the right to sell Hooters items in grocery stores. We're putting together a Hooters movie and even a casino. Hooters of America, based in Atlanta, owns the trademark and franchise licensing rights, along with the Hooters airline. The two groups have fought some well-publicized battles over the years, but the Fun Is Good mentality has endured throughout the chain.

In our office, which is located behind the original Hooters, we never take ourselves too seriously. That whimsical, creative attitude not only allows us to have fun but also keeps the ideas flowing. They must be pretty good because they're often copied.

Not long after we came up with the Hooters calendar, *Sports Illus-trated* produced one with their swimsuit models. One year we added a 3-D centerfold and included 3-D glasses. *SI* did the same the following year.

Hooters celebrated its 20th anniversary in 2003 and, like any mature business, the challenge is to maintain the attitude and creativity from the early years while recognizing that you're all grown up.

We encourage employees to be themselves, interact with customers, and have fun. If you're not having fun, you're doing it wrong. It starts with hiring. We try to hire people who are spontaneous and have a sense of humor. Our creative people are a bunch of nuts. The pranks flow freely, and even the boss is not off limits.

In our old office, employees got into the habit of feeding squirrels peanuts near an outside planter. It was funny at first, and the employees even named a couple of the cute squirrels "Carl" and "Stubby." Before long, dozens of squirrels were appearing for feedings. When a rat showed up, I put my foot down. No more feeding the squirrels.

The next day there was a sign posted in the planter. "Down with Ed." It was signed "Carl and Stubby." For Christmas, I received a calendar picturing rats. Before we moved, we placed a sign in the window so people would know where to find us. Someone put a sign in the planter on behalf of Carl and Stubby. "We're moving, too."

Our break room includes designated space for a keg of beer, along with a sign that says "Lobby Bar." After all, a hotel lobby bar often is the place everyone meets during conventions. Every office should have some sort of relaxed gathering place.

Many people think our new building looks like a high school. We heard it so often that we ran with it, placing a banner in the entryway. "Dance in the gym tonight."

Corporate cultures are screaming for this kind of mentality. Half of the people in business today don't recognize that fun is a key element of success, let alone that it's not hard to create.

If you start looking for ways to be irreverent, you'll find they're all around you. I used to be the vice chairman of special events for the Clearwater Chamber of Commerce. One of the board members always introduced me by saying, "And now Ed will present a report that a trained chimpanzee can give."

I bit my tongue and played along, until one day I discovered a woman who trained chimpanzees. At the next monthly meeting, my last running special events, I announced that someone else would be giving the report.

The chimp walked in wearing a T-shirt that read "vice chairman of special events." The animal jumped into my chair, started shuffling papers, and the place went crazy. The harder they laughed, the more animated the chimp became. It was a bargain for $100.

I paid the trainer more money to bring it back to my office, where it had a similar impact. You can't overestimate the importance of this in the workplace. If you have a boring job, stunts like these mix things up. It's a 20-minute stimulation that makes the entire day exciting.

It's the difference between people telling their spouses, "You're never going to believe what happened at work today," instead of "same old, same old."

With the talent pool so lean, employees are going to demand a fun, creative place to work. Before Hooters, I worked for a major home-builder. The boss was a tough, serious guy who liked a good joke, but there were limits. I was always pulling stuff, learning that if you're conscious of the parameters, you can have fun with anyone.

The Fun Is Good lessons are so valuable because there's no shortage of serious, critical issues in society, and we need a break. We need laughter and twists in our lives to serve as antidotes for all of the things that drain us mentally and physically.

It starts with never missing an opportunity to be irreverent. You'll start to look at things with a mischievous grin and your head cocked to the side, wondering what you can do with a sunken boat or a trained chimpanzee. You'll find such opportunities impossible to resist and come to understand how invaluable they are to growing your business and making it fun for employees and customers.

Just don't be surprised to find yourself wearing a chicken suit.

• •

FUN IS GOOD

Chapter 6 Summary and Exercises (The Power of Irreverence)

- Everyone wants to laugh at work.
- A lack of irreverence can cause a company to lose employees and customers.
- Don't be afraid to poke fun at yourself or your company.
- Everyone should feel comfortable suggesting ideas, no matter how outlandish.
- A dartboard or Nerf basketball hoop can work wonders in the office.
- Every office needs a few "good clubhouse" people to keep things loose.
- Successful companies are viewed as irreverent.
- Highly successful companies cultivate that atmosphere internally.
- Promote a Casual Friday environment, not just a dress code.
- Current events provide an endless stream of inspiration for irreverence.
- What three things can you do in the next week to create irreverence in your office?
- How can you apply current events to have fun at work?

Chapter 7

The Business of Laughter

When I was growing up, my family held fire drills. I'm one of nine children, so it was important that we have a plan for getting everyone out of the house in an orderly fashion.

One child was designated to grab the "idea box," an old wooden container that was full of index cards, cocktail napkins, and matchbook covers with ideas scribbled on them. We didn't have a safe and rarely had any money lying around, but that's beside the point. When you're 10 years old and you're having a fire drill—theoretically to save your butt—you're thinking, "There must be something really valuable about ideas."

That made a profound impression on me. Companies need to place the same value on ideas, no matter how outlandish or who came up with them. Companies cannot grow unless there's a steady flow of creative ideas coming from all corners of the business. The chiefs must be receptive to this and empower employees to implement exciting new programs.

Too often, that's not the case. More typical is the middle manager, the "memo king," whose job seems to be to preserve the status quo. You know the type. He sends memos constantly, hasn't had an original idea in his life, and avoids taking any responsibility for failures. Have a success, however, and he can't take enough credit.

The memo king doesn't believe in taking a risk, so he hires people who think just the way he does and makes sure nothing ever changes.

Employees have a right to have their opinions valued. I'm not suggesting a takeover, but try to get your message heard. If you work for a company that doesn't value your opinion, then they don't respect you. Move on to someplace else.

Employees need to keep pushing. They need to go to their supervisors and say there should be more fun here. You should try these ideas not simply because it will make the workplace more enjoyable, but because it's good for business.

Chris Sullivan and Bob Basham once worked for the Steak and Ale restaurant chain and Norman Brinker, one of the great restaurant entrepreneurs of all time. When Pillsbury purchased Steak and Ale in 1976, it evolved into a place where ideas and creativity no longer flourished. The entrepreneurial spirit died. Steak and Ale became bureaucratic, with plenty of memo kings.

Sullivan and Basham decided to go off elsewhere and try their ideas themselves. They were involved with Chili's in its early days and later launched Outback Steakhouse, a chain that has taken the casual steakhouse concept light years beyond Steak and Ale.

The moral of this story, of course, is that it's wise to look to your employees for ideas. If not, they might move on and come back to haunt you. If you're the employee, don't take no for an answer more than three times.

In Tampa, where Sullivan and Basham founded Outback, they're known as "The Outback Boys." I love that title. It makes them sound like some tough-as-nails, renegade country band. Next time you're thinking about whether to entertain a radical idea or escape the corporate bureaucracy, think of The Outback Boys.

You want to foster an atmosphere where employees believe that their ideas are valued and that anything is possible. Ideally, the chiefs are on board with this, but even if they're not, it's possible to launch the transformation from middle management or even the rank-and-file level.

Southwest Airlines thrives because its chairman, Herb Kelleher, embraces the Fun Is Good attitude. He's the ringleader of the circus, and it trickles down. I imagine it's easy to throw out ideas in that company and know they won't be automatically brushed aside.

If you're a chief ready to change the culture, you can pull it off just by explaining how and why it's going to be done. Ask employees for their input. Pass out copies of this book. Buy a copy of our video training series. The company must believe in the power of change.

Once you have that, it's time to externalize the process. Get your customers, suppliers, and vendors involved by soliciting their ideas. Delivery people and other visitors should be able to sense a change in your business.

The reason laughter is such good business is that people want to deal with companies that are having fun. A Fun Is Good company can articulate what makes their business different from the one down the street that provides the same service or product. They're having fun and making their company fun to their customers in dozens of little ways.

If you're a middle manager or employee, try to find some like-minded colleagues to start the process. Once you change the attitude of the office, as discussed in Part I, it should be easy to try new ideas. If not, take the approach of The Outback Boys and go somewhere else.

The best way to measure the potential for Fun Is Good is to hold a contest. When I joined the Detroit Tigers before the 2002 season, I challenged employees to give me their best ideas to improve the company. I was especially interested in promotions and marketing ideas that we could spring on our customers to generate fun and excitement. The author of the best idea would win a trip to Hawaii. Second place was a cruise to Bermuda, and third place was an all-expenses-paid trip to Las Vegas, gambling money not included.

The contest generated about 80 great ideas. It also showed that about half the workforce had the Fun Is Good mindset; about 30 percent actually participated in the contest. The winner used the Hawaii trip as his honeymoon, and people were ecstatic for him because it made the contest seem legitimate. I've always found that luxury trips are far greater incentives than cash prizes, probably because the cash is just used to pay bills. The trip is remembered forever.

Within all employees are budding entrepreneurs. Maybe they never make the jump, but in the back of their minds they're always coming up with ideas of how they'd run the company if given the chance. With a contest, they get their opportunity.

Did the contest in Detroit cost us? Sure, although even then we managed to swap some tickets and sponsorships for the travel deals. Even if we had paid cash for the trips, the ideas generated would have paid it back and then some. More importantly, I got a feel for who was receptive to Fun Is Good.

I bring this up because I know there are skeptics who believe Fun Is Good will not work for their offices. Perhaps it sounds unrealistic. In reality, they believe, people are more concerned with getting by day to day. They have families, mortgages, and responsibilities. No one has time to create ideas and introduce fun to the workplace.

Maybe, you figure, it works for minor league baseball, but how will it work in the worlds of law, medicine, insurance, or consulting?

There's not one organization, one profession, where Fun Is Good won't work. Maybe you're a manager who has inherited an office with no pulse, a group of beaten-down corporate drones. Maybe you're an employee who has just joined such a place.

It doesn't matter. There's a chink in the armor somewhere. I always make it a point to get waiters to laugh, especially when I get a server who clearly is not in the mood. If I can brighten his or her day, I might get better service. Even if I don't, it's worth a try.

The same is true in the office. Successful companies know that laughter—in the form of irreverence, hustling, customer service with a smile, and a constant flow of crazy promotional ideas—is their lifeblood. We've talked about a few of them, such as Southwest Airlines, Hooters, and SPAM. Anyone—and I mean anyone—can follow their lead by coming up with a few simple ideas.

Let's say you're a law firm. Everyone knows a few good lawyer jokes. Poke fun at yourself. Invite the public to submit their best jokes, with the winners receiving some free basic service like help with a will or incorporation. Team up with some local "morning zoo" radio show to offer legal advice on the air. Listeners who ran afoul of the law over the weekend can call in Monday morning and spill their guts to "Alex Smith, an attorney from Dewey, Cheatum, and Howe."

Let's say you're a plumber. Nobody is the, ahem, butt of more jokes than plumbers. There's plumber's crack and the griping about how much plumbers cost, especially when your toilet explodes late on a Saturday night. Why not play off that? Announce a flat one-price rate that's slightly less expensive than the competition.

Let's say you're a funeral home. Offer a free prepaid funeral to the person who comes up with the most creative way they'd like to be eulogized and remembered. We actually did this in Charleston, teaming up with a local funeral home. Like many of our promotions, we thought it was borderline tasteless, but fans got into it. Seniors, in particular, wrote elaborate, heartfelt funeral plans. We earned some critical acclaim and won some awards for that one—ironic for a group that's often had to answer to the Catholic Church or some other offended party because of similar gags.

Let's say you run a landscaping service. Do some semi-clandestine random acts of beauty. Ask local schools if you can redo an entryway right where parents leave their children off, and post a little sign that says, "Landscaping donated and installed by Acme Nurseries." Team up with a radio station to stage a contest where listeners phone in with the ugliest public areas. There's probably some street corner that once looked beautiful but now the flowers are dead and the planters are filled with cigarette butts.

Let's say you're selling home sites for a new community. Why not stage the world's largest Easter egg hunt over all that vacant land?

Perhaps you run an insurance agency. Sponsor every Little League in town by purchasing an outfield wall sign. I know several underwriters who do this, and they struggle to keep up with all of the business it generates. This might seem more like common sense than creative promotion, but it's amazing how many companies ignore these simple opportunities.

Let's say you run a mom-and-pop sandwich shop, a tough gig these days with Subway popping up on every corner. It's a lot like minor league baseball in that you have to immerse yourself in the community to be successful. Do this by creating coupons and promotions with schools, youth sports leagues, and churches.

You can market anything and make it fun. During my ad agency days at Wexler, McCarron & Roth, we had a men's clothing store as a client. When you think of hip, irreverent companies, men's clothing stores don't generally come to mind.

For Dale Alan, a men's clothier in South Florida, we created a billboard that was a coupon. Anyone who redeemed this 14-by-48-foot coupon was entitled to a free suit. We basically dared people to take down the billboard.

Sure enough, four buddies who had served in Vietnam together staged a covert operation in the middle of the night and dismantled our billboard. The following day we got a call from the ringleader who wanted to make sure that it was, indeed, a valid promotion and that they weren't going to be arrested.

We assured him that he would get his free suit and that no charges would be filed. We asked only that he show up with the sign at Dale Alan at around 4:00 in the afternoon, which would be good timing for evening news crews.

Dale Alan received 2 days of priceless media exposure for the cost of a suit, along with some billboard repair charges. Not only that, but South Florida recognized the store as hip and bold instead of old and stodgy.

For another Dale Alan billboard, we made it look like the painter had fallen off the scaffolding. The paint can was hanging upside down and the brush mark from the "n" trailed off the billboard. People pulled over to see if the painter was okay, only to discover the can nailed to the billboard. Ultimately the Department of Transportation made us take down the billboard, thus proving that a promotion can be *too* successful.

These kinds of cheap theatrics normally are associated with new companies and grand openings, but Dale Alan was an established business in South Florida. Company officials recognized that the most effective way to grow their business was through laughter.

No matter what your business, take a look at what you do and who your customer base is, and find a way to promote and better serve customers through laughter and joy.

There's a mom-and-pop convenience store near my home that keeps a huge cooler of Nehi sodas near the cash register. It's hard for anyone, especially those of us over a certain age, to resist grape and orange Nehi in bottles. They probably sell four cases of it a day because they recognize it brings people back to a more simple time.

Lawyer Appreciation Day

It seems everyone loves making fun of lawyers. Inspired by an idea from my fellow co-owner Marv Goldklang, a highly successful businessman who is sometimes accused—quite unfairly—of being a stuffy guy, we created an entire promotion out of lawyer jokes for the Canaries, our team in Sioux Falls, South Dakota.

We called it "Lawyer Appreciation Day," and the goal was to raise as much money as possible for charitable legal defense funds by making fun of attorneys. We charged lawyers double the admission price for a ticket, and billed them every three innings for concession items. A season-ticket-holding judge donned his robe and set up a makeshift courtroom along the right field line. People with real or imagined disputes were given a few minutes to plead their case, and the judge issued binding decisions.

The team mascot, a canary, invited lawyers to dance on the dugout roof between innings, and at the end of the game fans voted for the worst dancing lawyer. All told, we raised several thousand dollars for charity. Peter Jennings mentioned it on ABC's *World News Tonight*.

We held Lawyer Appreciation Day during my brief stint with the Tampa Bay Devil Rays, and it, too, was successful, though the head of one of the local bar associations wrote an angry letter. Apparently, he didn't like having his profession ridiculed.

I guess some lawyers can't take a joke.

• •

I know another guy who sells auto parts. He compiles lists of his clients' birthdays and delivers birthday cakes when he goes on sales calls. It livens up the office, brings some joy and laughter, and inevitably he leaves with an order. Sometimes he doesn't, but that's okay because people associate him with laughter. It's good for business.

The cakes seem like random acts of kindness, even if there's a smart strategy behind them. Karma tends to play a big role in business.

After all, people identify the guy as someone who enjoys his work, and they want to be around him more. Not only that, but humor aids in the exchange of information. If you take a button-down, perfunctory approach to your work, you won't get nearly as far.

When you approach customers and they see that you enjoy yourself and bring joy and laughter to their workplace, you learn valuable things about the client. Perhaps they're opening a new store. They're having trouble in a certain area or looking to bolster a part of the sales force. Maybe that information directly helps your business. Maybe it doesn't, but you can put them in touch with someone who may be able to help.

These kinds of informal exchanges serve as the most effective research you can conduct. Most companies think of research in terms of telephone surveys, focus groups, and outside consultants, when it's really as simple as asking your customers, vendors, and colleagues for their opinions. Companies pay millions of dollars when they could be getting more effective results for free.

It's the little things that separate the companies that succeed from those that fail. One of my most rewarding experiences was when a fan in St. Paul came up to me following a post-game fireworks show and thanked me profusely. He understood that the fireworks probably cost more than we took in that night, but the point was it made a difference to our customers.

· ·

Easter at the Ballpark

When I was with the Chicago White Sox in the late 1970s, we staged a massive Easter egg hunt at Comiskey Park. I didn't think this up very far in advance, and we ended up working around the clock boiling and dyeing thousands of eggs in preparation for the kids who would arrive before the next day's game. Roy Rivas, the wonderful White Sox chef, has never forgotten what I put him through. I can't say I blame him.

The spectacle of hundreds of kids storming the field in search of Easter eggs made for great television and, not surprisingly, the Chicago media came out in force. To keep things orderly, we decided to allow just 500 kids onto the field.

Parents revolted. Many began lifting their children down over the walls onto the field. This also made for great television, though thankfully (unlike Disco Demolition) it did not cause a disturbance.

As many youth sports leagues have learned in recent years, it's the behavior of adults, not the children, that causes trouble.

· ·

The most effective way to keep ideas flowing is to give credit publicly, both in the office and outside. Announce to your staff that Stacy had a fabulous idea. Give her a gift certificate to a restaurant or a day off.

If your company is the type that receives media coverage, make sure that person is identified. Many companies don't do this. They have designated spokespeople, and only they can speak to the media. Either that or the boss takes the credit for everything.

Let the people responsible for the success talk with the media.

I've been in the promotions racket for so long that people assume any silliness our teams conjure up must have come from me. These days, that's rarely the case.

In 2004, two of our employees in St. Paul came up with a brilliant promotion. Matt Hansen and Eban Yeager decided to use eBay to auction off the chance to bat for the Saints in a preseason game, with the proceeds going to charity.

Marc Turndorf, a 35-year-old video game producer, paid $5,601. When the media called me looking for comments, I directed them to Matt and Eban, or at least gave them credit. This kind of public acknowledgment often means more than money.

A good chief shares the credit for successful ideas and falls on the sword for the ones that bomb. That requires the courage to let employees run with ideas, even if you have reservations.

That's why I'm proud of Vasectomy Night. It began when a group of female employees of our Charleston RiverDogs team came to me and said they had a great idea for a promotion. Like most men, I cringed and instinctively brought my knees together. But they were serious. Give it away on Father's Day, they suggested. It would all be very tasteful. It wouldn't be a problem.

We announced the promotion early one afternoon, figuring it might generate a smattering of media interest. Within an hour, we had heard from the Catholic archdiocese and Charleston Mayor Joseph Riley. Not long thereafter, Bud Selig called the president of the National Association, which is the governing body of minor league baseball, to order the promotion canceled. Back then, Bud was just the acting commissioner as opposed to the actual commissioner, but he still carried a lot of weight. By the end of the afternoon, we had canceled the promotion, but not before the media had picked up the story. In heavily Catholic towns such as Philadelphia and Baltimore, the reception was terrible. We were shredded in the papers. The devil himself had taken over the Charleston RiverDogs.

Was the promotion a bit over the top? Perhaps. Then again, it could have been an instance of people taking things too seriously. I was raised Catholic, so I think I understand the concerns of the Catholic Church. But I took the blame, and the story dissipated quickly. I still believe it was a good idea, and it never would have been brought to light if we had not empowered our people.

If nothing else, the promotion generated my all-time favorite newspaper headline: "Promotion Snipped."

When you do something wrong, admit it and move forward. We're always thinking in terms of, "My God, if I do this, it will end my career." Look, I've ended my career several times, and things always work out. The truth is that we take ourselves way too seriously. I would rather err on the side of laughter than on the side of being too stiff.

I took the heat for Vasectomy Night because the same employees who suggested it also came up with countless others that were successful.

Empower your employees. Workplaces should be fun, and people need to be empowered and know that they are free to make decisions. Your business won't grow because you're a control freak; it will grow only if people are free to make decisions.

Too often, good ideas become lost in corporate bureaucracy. An employee is told meetings are needed to discuss it. Maybe next year, if the budget is right, even if the idea doesn't cost a thing.

A good company rubber-stamps ideas and empowers employees to execute them. When those employees are successful, they get all of the credit. After all, if the company is going to get all of the benefit, at least let the employee take a few moments to bask in the glow.

• •

Baseball Pinball

I've yet to implement my greatest idea ever. I want to replace Dad's exploding scoreboard with something more modern. Dad's not around to one-up me, of course, but he would applaud me for my tireless hustling.

I want to turn the baseball diamond into the equivalent of a pinball machine. When a player hits a home run, he will set off a 20-second cycle of craziness. A motorized marching band will rise up from behind the right field wall and proceed on a track to right-center field. The "Hallelujah Chorus" will ring out. Ten cannons will blast confetti into the stands. Chase lights will be activated along the outfield wall. Fog machines will be involved.

Best of all, when the batter rounds the bases, he'll activate smoke machines. When he steps on first base, he'll trigger a mechanism that produces red smoke. Yellow smoke will come from second base; green from third. I've had this designed, and the same folks who produced

Phantom of the Opera contributed the smoke effects. The entire production would cost about $1 million, but as any good hustler knows, the goal is to get someone else to pay for it.

In 1999, during my brief tenure with the Tampa Bay Devil Rays, I cut a deal with Tropicana to sponsor this little black magic box I called pinball baseball. It was to revolutionize the game.

After I left, the deal broke down. The Rays ultimately created a huge orange that lit up after home runs, and the catwalks of the domed building were rigged with lights, but it wasn't the same.

My partners in the minor leagues no doubt would help pay for it, but you've probably guessed by now that I'd take more joy out of it by finding a sponsor to foot the bill. Not just because it wouldn't cost me anything, but also because I'd like to see some progressive company benefit.

Anyone interested?

· ·

Fun Is Good Vignette

Melissa McCants,
Director of Sports Marketing, College of Charleston

"I called it "Cow Bingo." The idea was to mark off a large athletic field into squares, raffle 300 spaces for $100 apiece, and bring in a cow. Wherever the "chip" fell determined the winner."

This was the type of Fun Is Good idea that Mike would have rubber-stamped quickly during my time working for his Charleston RiverDogs baseball team. But the folks at the College of Charleston, mirroring the conservative attitudes of the surrounding community, were not as receptive.

For 3 years, I took the idea to my boss; for 3 years he turned it down. He worried that we'd offend donors or athletic department sponsors or that it would be beneath the dignity of the college to have a cow soiling school property.

To his credit, he finally gave in the following year. Between raffle tickets and event sponsorship, we netted $30,000 for our scholarship fund once the $10,000 prize had been awarded.

The contest was a huge success, even though the cow took forever to get down to business. In the meantime, we awarded prizes—such as gallons of "Holy Cow" ice cream—to the owners of squares the cow visited for at least 15 minutes. Besides Cow Bingo, there was an all-you-can-eat oyster roast. We charged $25 admission.

Because of the positive feedback, my boss insisted we make Cow Bingo an annual event, which is ironic considering I might have gotten in trouble had the contest flopped or we received a negative response. I suppose that's a risk you take in implementing Fun Is Good.

I give him credit for giving me the green light. Admittedly, it took persistence on my part, but that's what it takes sometimes to bring about a change in attitudes in workplaces accustomed to doing things a certain way.

Maybe you're wondering if Fun Is Good could work with your company or be applied to your career. I had my doubts at first. Even though the College of Charleston is a neighbor of the Charleston RiverDogs, it was light years away in some respects. Perhaps your workplace is stodgy, with little progressive thinking.

When I was struggling with bringing Fun Is Good to my new employer, I asked Mike what I should do. "If you believe in your idea, put your full effort into it, and are willing to take responsibility for it should it fail, you have nothing to worry about," he said.

That's good advice—not just for Cow Bingo, but for career planning as well. I'm in collegiate sports marketing not because it has a tremendous financial upside but because I have the opportunity to have fun at my job.

In my field, I have the chance to show people a great time. If they can walk away from Cow Bingo or a similar event happy, then I've done my job, and I take great pride in that.

For me, Fun Is Good means that no matter what your age, there's still that kid deep down inside looking to get out. I've been guided by that notion, that with a little determination and chutzpah, anything is possible.

Maybe things won't always work out, though I'm willing to take that risk as long as I believe in the idea and put my full effort behind it.

If I've done that, then I'm comfortable letting the chips fall where they may.

. . . .

FUN IS GOOD

Chapter 7 Summary and Exercises (The Business of Laughter)

- Creative ideas and promotions are the lifeblood of any successful organization.
- Good ideas come from everyone, not just the chiefs.
- Employees who don't have their ideas heard should look elsewhere for work.
- Any company can benefit from off-the-wall promotion.
- Hold employee contests for ideas.
- What three promotions could help your company?
- How can your career or business benefit from "random" acts of kindness?
- Give credit to those who deserve it. If you signed off on an idea, take the blame if it fails.

Chapter 8

Embracing Failure

I f an idea works, it's not a big deal. But if it fails, it makes a great after-dinner speech.

That's not just a line. People prefer to hear about colossal flameouts rather than modest successes, and I have several keynote speeches that focus on my failures. As you can imagine, they touch upon Disco Demolition and my well-publicized struggles with the Tampa Bay Devil Rays.

Of course, Disco Demolition launched me into a decade of despair, and my stint with the Devil Rays coincided with my daughter's diagnosis and early dealings with retinitis pigmentosa. I wouldn't wish those experiences on anyone.

But I use Disco Demolition and my Rays days to illustrate that it's not only okay to fail; it's imperative. Too many companies and individuals refuse to take chances because they're afraid to fail. As a result, they never grow.

This happens in workplaces all the time. Someone will suggest something progressive and it will be dismissed automatically, usually by some middle manager who believes it's his job to preserve the status quo. After all, it's worked before. Why mess with success? We have too much on the line! What if we fail?

What if you succeed? What if this unusual suggestion sparks change and growth in your company? What if one of your competitors thinks of it first? You can't afford not to risk failure.

Ask any group of executives what they think of change, and they'll sing its virtues. They love change. Change is good. We can't grow without change. Yet when it comes to executing change, everyone gets skittish. No one wants to risk failure.

It's okay to fail. I've failed numerous times, with the details often chronicled in the newspapers. I'd always rather go down failing while attempting a change for the better than succeed at preserving the status quo.

Admitting failure is one of life's most difficult things. It's uncomfortable even to talk about it. My only poignant speech is about failure. The audience will grow uncomfortably silent, and not just because they were expecting Mike Veeck to spin his hilarious tales from the world of minor league baseball promotions.

They become quiet because it's so unusual to talk about it. Whenever I give that speech, I sit back down to dinner and, without fail, I start receiving notes. Many come from men, who seem even more uncomfortable with failure than women.

People are terrified of failure, to the point where they become immobilized. They stay in jobs for far too long because they're afraid of what might happen if they quit and try something new. They give up on dreams without ever trying simply because they're terrified of failing.

It's easier to play it safe, to stay the course in a career you don't particularly like, because the devil you do know is better than the one you don't. The fear of failure is that powerful.

I've failed many times, in several cases in spectacular public fashion. I spent most of my 30s wallowing in self-pity, despair, and alcohol. I was deep in debt at the age of 40.

My most memorable "failure" came on July 12, 1979. As promotions director for the White Sox, I teamed up with Chicago deejay Steve Dahl and decided to blow up some disco records in a dumpster between games of a twi-night doubleheader between the Detroit Tigers and Chicago White Sox. We had a younger crowd on hand that evening, and the smell of marijuana wafted through the grandstands.

This was not a typical baseball crowd. Most of these kids probably didn't know Bill Veeck from Mr. Bill. This was the Woodstock they never had.

At the end of the first game, kids who could not get into the ballpark grew impatient. Old Comiskey Park had portable ticket booths, and the kids began rocking them. We sent a chunk of the security force to deal with it, leaving the field virtually unguarded.

After we blew up the records, a few kids slid down the foul poles onto the field. Others came over the wall. Shards of shattered records rained down like vinyl shrapnel. Some news reports would call it a riot, but in truth it was relatively peaceful because most of the kids were stoned. Had it been a crowd of drunken baseball fans, we really would have had a problem.

Nevertheless, the umpires determined that the field was unplayable, and the White Sox were forced to forfeit the second game, just the fourth-ever forfeit in big league history.

The Chicago newspapers devoted a staggering amount of space to Disco Demolition, an amount usually reserved for the beginnings of war or natural disasters. Dad and I were ripped relentlessly, though

Dad put things in the proper perspective. "The promotion worked too well," he told me.

Dad took a lot of blame for a promotion he had nothing to do with, and I felt horribly guilty about it. I hung around the White Sox for another 7 months, but the fun was gone, especially when it became evident that the new era of free agency had made it next to impossible for low-budget operators like my dad to compete.

In 1980, at the age of 29, I resigned from the White Sox, figuring I'd get five or six offers to work in baseball. But the phone never rang. I heard from radio stations, soccer teams, and other places that wanted to tap into my semi-controlled chaos, but nobody from baseball was interested.

A friend of mine from South Florida invited me to come live in the sunshine and work for his construction company. I had just gotten married, and the two of us moved to Fort Lauderdale, where I began working with my hands for the first time. I didn't want to learn construction so much as I wanted to get away from Chicago and the phones that were not ringing.

Hanging drywall is lonely work. You're alone with your thoughts and an incessant drilling sound, and it's a wonderful way to clear your head. After a while, I was bored and started visiting the jai alai fronton in Dania. I was mesmerized by the speed and the agility of these athletes coupled with this unique packaging of sport and pari-mutuel betting. I figured I could apply some of the same magic that I had watched Dad bring to Suffolk Downs.

Having nailed enough sheetrock, I applied to become the promotions manager for the fronton. Nobody expected much. People in the pari-mutuel business figured their audience was those interested only in gambling, not ancillary promotions.

For the next year, I dusted off my cheap theatrics. We held concerts, dabbled with indoor pyrotechnics, and brought in various B-list celebrities to draw crowds. Attendance soared, and Dania jai alai became an event.

One day I discovered 800 old uniform tops in a storage closet. I sent them out to be dry-cleaned and announced a promotion in which we would give fans the shirts off our backs. People lined up around the building to get a jersey. Unless anyone else wants to take credit, I believe that promotion inspired similar giveaways that now are commonplace throughout sports.

We had some fun at Dania jai alai, but it was a very corporate environment. In what would become a familiar pattern in my latter incarnation in Major League Baseball, I felt stifled in a corporate culture full of memos and meetings.

Then I ran into three guys who would change my life. Jerry Wexler, Mel Roth, and Bob McCarron ran an advertising agency that handled the Dania jai alai account. Not long after I was hired, I went to lunch with the three of them, ostensibly to let them know their services were no longer needed.

After all, this is what a new marketing guy does: He brings in his own guys. I didn't have any guys, but I knew I had to get some. Instead, I was mesmerized by these three fellows who brought a self-deprecating attitude to the meeting. They knew they were going to be let go but never lost their sense of humor.

Instead, they became my guys, to the point where I left the fronton after a year and went to work for the Wexler, McCarron & Roth agency. For the next 6 or 7 years, I toiled as an account executive, crafting ads and injecting Fun Is Good into companies that were anything but irreverent. I learned from these talented guys how effective Fun Is Good advertising can be, valuable knowledge I later would take back to baseball.

Unfortunately, I never stopped drinking. It always had been recreational in Chicago, where hard drinking went hand-in-hand with the culture of baseball. My Dad drank a case of beer a day, holding court into the wee hours at some saloon or in the Bard's Room, a gathering spot in the bowels of great old Comiskey Park where sportswriters, managers, and other baseball guys would down beer and argue about baseball long after the game had ended.

In Florida, there was a darker, self-pitying side to my drinking. I added cocaine to the mix. As much as I was enjoying my gig at WM&R, my self-worth was nonexistent. I blamed it on being out of baseball, but it went much deeper. It was an inability to know my place in the world. I wondered how much of the White Sox experience had been mine. For how much of it was I responsible, as opposed to my dad? I knew I was a driving force in that club, but the lack of job offers didn't validate that.

It didn't help that I wasn't mentioned in an epilogue chronicling Dad's second stint as White Sox owner that appeared in a new version of Dad's first book, *Veeck as in Wreck*. Dad sold the White Sox to Jerry Reinsdorf and Eddie Einhorn for $22 million in 1981, twice what Dad had paid for the club, and I had felt I had at least a partial hand in that.

The year 1986 began on a bad note when Dad died on January 2. My son was born on April 11, but even that couldn't prop me up. There was some vague talk of my being part of an ownership group to buy the San Diego Padres, but that went nowhere. It didn't matter; I had no money. Even my dad, who took the creative financing of ball clubs to the level of art form, had always had some personal funds.

I sent letters to every club in baseball asking for an interview. Roland Hemond and Dave Dombrowski, well-connected baseball men and dear friends, intervened on my behalf. But nobody wanted to hire a Veeck, especially not a drunk Veeck.

Then I was turned down for a partnership at Wexler, McCarron & Roth, where I had labored for 7 years. It wasn't so much the ownership position itself as it was that I needed the assurance that I was reliable and that my life wasn't spinning out of control. I needed some validation from the outside world but didn't get it from "my guys."

I left on the spot and started my own agency. I picked up a client here and there, but I could not have been that creative. I was out all night, most every night, and gassed most of the time. I suffer from an irregular heartbeat, and one day about a month before my son was born, my heart just stopped. While recovering in the hospital room, a doctor walked by and looked at my charts.

"You VEEK?" he asked, in a thick Eastern European accent.

I nodded.

"You eat red meat 5 days a week?"

"Yes, I do."

"You drink a bottle of whiskey a day?"

I nodded. The charts told no lies.

"Beer too?"

"Yes."

"You'll be lucky to see your child to the age of 2."

The doctor shook his head and left. He wasn't even my doctor, just a guy who dealt with clowns like me all day long. I was just another jerk who wasn't going to listen.

Rock bottom came about a year later, after my wife and I had separated. I was driving back and forth along Atlantic Boulevard in Fort Lauderdale, drunk and wallowing in self-pity.

A cop pulled me over. I wanted him to arrest me, but instead, he put me in a cab. Maybe the cop was being humane. Maybe he was about to get off his shift and didn't want to deal with me. Maybe he had been there before. Whatever the reason, he didn't do what I wanted him to do, which was arrest me, which would have taken things out of my control.

When the cab arrived home, it dawned on me that I had no money. I stumbled around the apartment looking for cash, scrounging through drawers and under cushions until I somehow came up with enough to send the driver on his way. Even in my drunken stupor, it occurred to me that I had no dignity left.

The next day I biked to the local chapter of Alcoholics Anonymous. I stood on the sidewalk along Dixie Highway for 4 hours, baking in the sun, unable to push myself inside. An elderly woman finally popped out.

"You're looking fairly well done on this side," she said. "Perhaps you'd like to come in and have a cup of coffee because you're going to burn to death out here."

Over the next 90 days, I attended 150 AA meetings. I never said a word other than my first name and just listened to people who were in my same sorry shape.

Admittedly, my approach to AA was unconventional. I did not drink for 3 years and never took a sponsor. After that, I would have a couple of beers or a glass of wine, but the hard stuff ended that day along Dixie Highway.

I threw myself into my work and started riding my bike 100 miles a week. I've visited psychiatrists through the years, but I've found the really helpful stuff comes from within. It comes from when you take hold of your life, stop whining and making excuses, and look at the rest of the world. It's not about you.

Part of the transformation was the birth of my son and realizing that someone loved me unconditionally. I had a fresh canvas, a blank sheet of paper, and I felt comfortable being a father. That started the healing process, along with Alcoholics Anonymous and being clear-headed for the first time in forever.

Laughter is the key to overcoming failure. Make fun of your fears. For a long time, I couldn't deal with Disco Demolition. I viewed it as a career debacle that could not be overcome. I had brought shame to the Veeck name and legacy. How ridiculous was that?

Then one day, while I was living on a couch in an old boarding-house as I tried to stay sober, I was flipping the channels and stumbled across some Disco Demolition footage. It was part of *Rolling Stone* magazine's 20-year retrospective on the history of rock 'n' roll. Disco Demolition was the closing scene in the first half of the program.

I realized that the event that I had long viewed as a huge failure had become a piece of legend. No longer did I need to apologize for Disco Demolition. A few years later, the Los Angeles Dodgers gave away baseballs to fans entering the game. Not surprisingly, the fans hurled the balls onto the field, and the Dodgers ended up forfeiting the game. Disco Demolition suddenly didn't look nearly so reckless.

I was no longer the only guy who ran into his own Waterloo. I learned the importance of taking ownership of your failures. Be proud of them because they represent courage, creativity, and the willingness to try new things. We're 25 years removed from Disco Demolition, and it's still brought up nearly every time I'm intro-duced as a speaker or mentioned in an article. I like to think I've done a few noteworthy things since, but that remains my defining moment.

I'm okay with that now because Disco Demolition is viewed no longer as a failure but as a piece of history. Failures become assets because we learn and grow from them. As for being a stain on the Veeck legacy, how arrogant was it for me to think that way? It barely warrants a historical footnote.

There's such an unfair stigma to being fired. Now, if the termination is a result of poor performance, a lousy work ethic, or bad attitude, that's one thing. But many times the firing is the result of a new regime, an economic downturn, or management that just doesn't get Fun Is Good.

Rejection is part of the human experience. We can be fired from relationships and family situations. Divorce is a form of firing.

We tend to think of firing as a huge watershed moment that will forever define us. It doesn't have to be that way: Musicians wear firings almost as a badge of honor. There's always a better band or one willing to work for less. Athletes and coaches know they're going to be fired because in sports you're quickly rendered too old or ineffective. Those who work in television and radio, with ever-changing formats, management, and ownerships, laugh about how many times they've been fired.

People in the workplace would be wise to adopt a similar attitude. It's not so horrible unless you let it wear on you. Firings often occur because management changes, and the only way to deal with it is by laughing about it.

We all know people who fall into the trap of taking themselves too seriously and letting themselves be defined by a job, title, position, or salary. They think, "Now that I'm the president, I'm going to be here forever." It doesn't work that way because it's an ever-changing landscape, and the only way to survive is to recognize that initially and have fun with it. Otherwise, it becomes devastating when the gig is taken away, and it can take a long time to recover.

It's a lot easier if you don't let the job define you. You want to be defined as a wonderful spouse, parent, friend, child, and all-around good person. After all, nobody looks back during their final moments on Earth at what a great career they had.

Recognize that a job doesn't last forever and, like those aforementioned musicians and athletes, you're probably going to be fired. Once you understand this, you're free to have as much fun with the gig and be as creative as you can be. You'll be better equipped to live in the moment and have fun, and that makes a huge difference in your life. When it's all over, instead of dwelling on the firing, you'll focus on what a great run you had.

If it takes some time to find your next job, don't worry about it. People are so afraid of having that gap in their résumés. When I interview people, I look for those gaps. I want to know what they did during that period. Did they start their own business? Even if it failed, they no doubt developed skills that could serve my organization.

Did they travel the world? Take cooking classes? Sit on the beach and read books? Work in telemarketing? Play in a rock-and-roll band? All of those things can be valuable. Look at those gaps in the résumé as assets, not failures. John Kuhn, who runs our ball club in Sioux Falls, South Dakota, had a tough time finding a job when he got out of college, so he spent 6 months watching classic movies. That's a valuable and enviable experience.

I used to think my 10 years out of baseball represented a huge gap. In reality, those skills I learned from the ad agency and the jai alai fronton—even hanging drywall—were tremendous assets.

Sobering up is a strange experience. All of those feelings you're afraid of, such as failure, bubble to the surface. Suddenly you have to deal with emotions you never faced while anesthetized by alcohol.

It's a tough process, but there comes a point in the middle of the night when you look out at the expanse of what your life has become and you can't kid yourself any longer. I was lucky enough to figure some of it out. Others aren't so fortunate. They fell into the abyss because they could not face these personal demons.

The point of all of this is to show that it's never too late to overcome a failure or to reinvent oneself. I lost 10 years of my life, prime earning years when my energy was high. Thankfully, I never had a job I hated. I enjoyed hanging drywall for a few months, promoting jai alai, and working at the ad agency. All of those experiences made me more effective at working in baseball.

I was 35 when I sobered up, 38 when I got a chance to get back into the career I loved. Marv Goldklang, part owner of the team, resurrected my baseball career. I took a job at the lowest rung of baseball, working for a Class-A minor league franchise in Pompano Beach, Florida, that had no affiliation with a Major League team.

It should have been a humbling experience for someone who had toiled in the big leagues. Instead, I was ecstatic to be there.

A lot of people approaching a 40th or 50th birthday take stock of their lives and don't like what they see. They beat themselves up over failures and become conservative in their decision-making processes, not wanting to fail again.

That's understandable. But if in that soul-searching process you identify the failure as not pursuing something that might have made you happy, it's time to get over that fear of failure. It's time to summon that courage to finally pursue a passion or a career change that will make you happy.

You might not like what your life has become, but I guarantee you it probably looks better than mine did at the back end of 30. And if I can pull off a reasonably successful second act, anyone can. I mean, I'm a nice enough fellow, but there's nothing exceptional at work here.

. . . .

Overcoming the Fear of Public Speaking

Nobody is afraid of public speaking. They're afraid of *failing* at public speaking.

I used to be one of those people. Unlike my Dad, who gave hundreds of speeches a year, I did not have that confidence at first. Sure, I had dealt regularly with the media while working for the White Sox, and, unbeknownst to me, I had become pretty savvy in my presentations as an advertising executive.

Not long after I went back to work in baseball running the Miami Miracle, I was asked to host a local television program. They asked months ahead of time and I gladly accepted; we were starved for publicity.

As the day approached, I became increasingly apprehensive. I started thinking up excuses. I could come down with an illness or a devastating back ailment.

Before I left for the show, I walked into the closet to find some clothes. The fear became so intense that I literally froze, unable to come out.

My future wife, Libby, found me in a closet. I was petrified.

"You can do this," she said. "This is the business you love. You are lucky to have this opportunity. So quit your whining and come out of the closet."

I had to take the first step, literally out of the closet. What I learned that night, other than being reminded of the unflinching support of a remarkable woman, was that it's easy to talk about something you're passionate about.

I struggled with speaking until I found my niche. People heard the Veeck name and they expected to hear 50 years of baseball stories that I didn't have. Eventually, I remembered what worked with the ad agency presentations. My background in music had taught me to chat with the audience between songs and ad-lib vignettes.

These days, I sometimes approach Dad's prolific standard for speaking engagements. I've discovered that laughter helps. Nothing is more flattering than being asked to speak to a group, and there's no better way to promote a business or impart some wisdom—but you have to be able to laugh at yourself. I still get nervous before every speech, and I recognize that some of my stories and jokes are going to bomb. Sometimes the crowd isn't going to respond at all.

Public speaking, like anything else, is something that can be improved with practice and preparation. Just remember that by getting up to speak, you've already overcome the fear of failure. It just takes one step.

Don't worry about the critics. Simply by getting up to speak, you've done something many people never summon the courage to attempt.

• •

If a milestone birthday or a series of failures has brought you to a crisis point, go back and look at family photos. Find some in which you were happy. What was going on in your life at that point? Can you recapture that?

Maybe you're looking at 40 or 50 and wondering how to make a change. For starters, stop and listen more. I spend a couple of hours a day on my bicycle listening to the sounds and taking in the smells. Most of us have to live at such a frenetic speed that we never get comfortable. The time on the bike has taught me that I can spend time with myself without obsessing over what's gone wrong.

Time can be the enemy that way. The challenge is to remove the self-centeredness from your world. Do some volunteer work, find a hobby, but whatever you do, shut up and stop talking about yourself. Nobody is interested. Follow the lead of Bill Veeck and talk to people about themselves. You'll learn more about yourself by listening to others.

Make a conscious effort to pursue what you *like* to do. Turn an avocation into a vocation. Think back to the times when life was good, and go off in pursuit of that.

Whether you realize it or not, we've all been buffeted by the hands of time and have a better idea of who we are. David Crosby calls it being more comfortable in your "meat suit." You're halfway through your life and you've learned a lot, even if it's by osmosis. Even if you've anesthetized yourself as I did, you still pick up a lot, and whatever it is, you can apply that to your current situation.

It can be difficult to make that jump. At the end of 1989, when I got that call from Marv Goldklang, I knew working in baseball was what I wanted to do. At the same time, I had just had a very profitable year at my ad agency. I still was about $50,000 in debt, dealing with child support payments, and had no business taking a job that paid $25,000 a year.

But I found a way to make it work. Even though I worked 15-hour days in baseball, I managed to handle a few advertising clients and cobble together sufficient income. Maybe you can do the same by keeping a few side gigs as you pursue something you really want to do.

As you can imagine, being given this second chance has had a great impact on me. For much of the '80s, I wrote letters to Major League Baseball teams asking for a job—any job. There was no interest, no phone calls, not even a form rejection letter.

Years later, when I made it back into baseball, at least at the minor league level, I got a call from a former big league executive who found himself out of work. He had ignored my queries all those years, but now he was looking for some direction.

You never know when fortunes will turn around, which is why I'm a sucker for second chances. In 1996, when Darryl Strawberry was banned from baseball for yet another drug-related offense, I had the opportunity to sign him to play for the St. Paul Saints (the Saints, as part of the independent Northern League, are not affiliated with major or minor league baseball and thus did not have to honor the ban).

Fans were outraged at the idea. They can forgive players for lots of transgressions, but squandering prodigious talent through drug use is not one of them. Even though fellow team owner Marv Goldklang and manager Marty Scott wanted to sign Darryl, I resisted. We had put forth all this effort to create a family-friendly environment. What message would signing Darryl send?

Still, I finally realized that I would have been a hypocrite for abandoning Darryl, so we brought him to St. Paul in 1996, and he enjoyed one of the happiest seasons of his career, playing for a tiny fraction of the salary he had earned in the majors. On July 1, we sold his contract to the New York Yankees, and he ended up on a team that won the World Series.

Darryl and I had a shared experience—and not just from abusing some of the same substances. For 10 years, all I wanted was one person to give me another chance in baseball, and nobody called.

That second chance has changed the approach I have today. Whenever I get a heartfelt letter from someone looking for a second chance—or struggling for a first—I try to help.

My job has become to make those people believe that there is a huge opportunity for them, and that those of us who have gone before are not exceptionally talented. We have harbored the same hopes and dreams, and I will open that door to anyone if I see a little glimmer of passion and I have the power to help.

Many people have dreams that they let die as they get older because they see them as logistically impossible. Younger people fall into this trap as well, giving up before they've really given it a chance.

In either case, it's not too late to get over this fear of failure. Remember, even failures can become popular after-dinner speakers.

· ·

Overcoming the Fear of Resignation

The fear of resigning often is scarier than the fear of being fired.

I've worked for four Major League Baseball teams, and in each case my tenure ended with resignation, even though it's been widely reported that I was fired in at least two of those instances. That reporting is not entirely inaccurate because I've often referred to my departures as firings—and not just because I was likely to be fired in at least one instance.

The reason I say I was fired is that it makes for a better story. After all, you can wear it as a badge of honor. It's also easier to assign the blame to someone else. You tend to beat yourself up more with resignations than firings.

People in bad work situations tend to do just enough to avoid being fired. They never resign because they're so afraid of the unknown. This is a huge mistake.

In 1998 and '99, I spent 7 months working for the Tampa Bay Devil Rays. It was a miserable experience working in a stifling, overly corporate environment where I did not fit.

Now, the Rays could argue quite convincingly that I also did not fit in during subsequent employment with the Florida Marlins and Detroit Tigers. I plead guilty as charged. But I refuse to give up on Major League Baseball, even if they have been slow to embrace Fun Is Good in the nearly 25 years since Dad sold the White Sox.

Still, I was reluctant to resign from the Devil Rays. I had waited 20 years for a second chance in Major League Baseball. I knew Tampa Bay wasn't a Fun Is Good place, but I was going to die trying to make it so.

My reaction is always to work harder; I can will this to happen. What I should have done was walk away immediately. I had become so miserable that when I came home, I had nothing left for my family. Every bit of joy I envisioned for that job had disappeared, and this happens across corporate America every day.

Some of my closest friends urged me not to resign. How could I quit after just 7 months? Now I would never get another shot at the majors, they said.

But there was a bigger stigma to staying. Leaving a job you dislike is not a big deal. I blamed myself for the failure, of course, but I was able to laugh about it the next day because I no longer defined myself by work.

Resignation is wrongly associated with quitting. When you resign, you're not giving up but *resigning* yourself to finding something better. Quitting is staying in a job that's making you miserable because you've given up hope.

If you're in a bad job, cut your losses and get out. Something better will come along. If you hang around and take the paycheck, you'll sap yourself of energy, lose a chunk of dignity, and get old in a hurry.

Whenever someone is fired or resigns, everyone in the office pities the person. What will become of her? Inevitably, a few months later you hear how this person is doing well in a new job. She's lost weight and seems like that cheerful gal everyone remembered from years ago.

It's because a firing or resignation is refreshing. It forces you to take stock of your life and puts you back in a position where you have tremendous enthusiasm and passion.

If anything, a firing or resignation gives you a clean slate. Sure, there might be some baggage attached, but you've no doubt learned from the experience and are stronger because of it.

So don't fear resignation. Be afraid of hanging around too long. Instead, resign yourself to something better.

· ·

FUN IS GOOD

Chapter 8 Summary and Exercises (Embracing Failure)

- Change isn't just good. It's a necessity.
- Don't take failures so seriously. Learn from them. Recognize them as assets.
- It's never too late to start over. Turn your avocation into a vocation.
- Laughter is the key to overcoming the fear of public speaking.
- Unless it's for poor performance, there's no shame in being fired.
- Offer second chances. You might need one yourself some day.
- Don't worry about gaps in a résumé. What did you learn during that time?
- Staying in a bad job saps energy and spirit. Get out as quickly as possible.
- You learn something valuable from every job.
- Resigning is not quitting. It's resigning yourself to something better.

Part III

· · · · · · · · · · · · · · · · · · ·

Spread the Word

NOW THAT YOU'VE examined the necessary mindset for Fun Is Good (Part I) and established a plan to apply Fun Is Good in your life (Part II), it's time to discuss how to make it a long-term solution and not just a short-term fix. A key idea behind Fun Is Good is that it's something to be shared, and we'll discuss the importance of mentoring and volunteering. It's also important to keep the magic of Fun Is Good alive, which is what we'll discuss in Chapter 9, "Every Day is Opening Day." In Chapter 10, we'll explore how Fun Is Good comes together to help you provide superior customer service. With the help of my daughter, Rebecca Veeck, we'll view Fun Is Good through the eyes of a child. Finally, I'll issue you a challenge to implement Fun Is Good in your career and workplace and let me know the results. By spreading Fun Is Good, you'll be amazed at how it comes back to you.

Chapter 9

Every Day Is Opening Day

One of the biggest challenges of any company is to keep the attitude and magic of the early days alive even as the business matures. The same is true from a career standpoint. It's easy to fall into routines and patterns, doing the same things year after year. Fun Is Good is easy to implement but tougher to maintain. If you can foster this magical atmosphere, you can keep the honeymoon period alive forever.

This is especially challenging for individuals who like what they do and companies that have achieved a degree of success. The problem is that if you don't continue to evolve and push yourself further, both from a company standpoint and as an individual, you're eventually going to grow stale.

Here, too, I can use our St. Paul Saints as an example. From the time we debuted in 1993 through about the 1997 season, we could do no wrong. We were the darlings of minor league baseball. Our attendance was 103 percent (I'm a sucker for letting people in who try to hustle me or have a sob story about how they drove 500 miles and couldn't get tickets). Each week, it seemed like a film crew from *60 Minutes* or HBO rolled into town looking to tell our story. On the field, we won three Northern League titles in the first five seasons.

How hot were we? There were instances where St. Paul Saints season tickets were left behind in wills and hotly contested in divorce court. There was a waiting list of more than 2,000 people for season tickets. We were on top of the world.

Unfortunately, I started to believe my own press and stopped pushing the envelope. Look at all these people filling our stadium! I must be a genius.

This happens in corporate America all the time. Companies that experience unbridled success think they don't need creative ideas anymore. It takes a talented person to ignore the praise and keep pushing the ideas and attitude that made them successful in the first place.

Success is a powerful narcotic. It's like the waves lapping against the side of the boat, so calming and peaceful that eventually you're lulled to sleep. It starts when you stop setting higher goals and trying to do new things. Why mess with success?

Some people see trouble coming and realize they have to change. But they figure they'll just milk the success for one more year and then address the problem. By then, often it's too late.

With the Saints, the first sign was when I agonized over signing Darryl Strawberry in 1996. In the Saints' early days, I thought nothing of signing Leon "Bull" Durham, a former big leaguer for the Chicago Cubs and St. Louis Cardinals who had battled drug problems. After all, I was a recovering addict and, according to my press, a guy who thrived on giving people second chances.

But when Darryl Strawberry needed a gig, I hesitated. We now were a mature company. Why rock the boat? Like a CEO of a young publicly held operation who worries about Wall Street and his shareholders and not what made the business successful in the first place, I was concerned about what the fans would think.

Thankfully, my wife, Libby, pointed out that I was acting like a hypocrite. The only reason I was with the Saints was that Marv Goldklang had been willing to believe in 1989 that I was no longer a drunk.

Darryl proved to be one of the greatest things to happen to the Saints in 1996. He had fun, served as a leader in the clubhouse, and brought some big league swagger to independent ball. He was a huge draw, signing autographs and laughing more than he had in years. He came to realize why he had loved baseball so much as a kid.

We pushed in other areas. We hired a group of local improvisational actors and put them to work in the stadium. They dressed in various costumes—a Samurai warrior, a magician, a hockey goalie named "The Sieve"—and made a dramatic entrance through the outfield before each game. We stole the concept from Cirque du Soleil, which has a cast member usher patrons to their seats. Our actors were part ushers, part cheerleaders, and part entertainers, working the crowd throughout the game. We didn't know what to call them until a newspaper writer referred to them as "ushertainers."

We had noticed that kids, the lifeblood of our business, were disappearing. A night at our ballpark had become a popular yuppie attraction. Come out with your friends and enjoy a few cheap beers in this eclectic atmosphere. There's nothing wrong with that, of course. But as our four professional sports leagues have proven, when you stop attracting families and children, you'll eventually struggle.

So we revamped our "Kid Zone" play areas. We even introduced a mascot, a big furry costume with a real person inside. I've always been a big fan of *real* animal mascots—each year in St. Paul we have a trained pig deliver baseballs to home plate, and in Fort Myers we have a trained dog perform the task—but I've never liked the idea of some young adult parading around in a cheesy, furry costume.

But kids love mascots. Dave Raymond, who for years played the wonderful Philadelphia Phillies mascot, "The Phanatic," reminded me of this. So I decided to try something new.

Finally, I did the most important thing to ensure that the St. Paul Saints did not grow stale and lose that Fun Is Good magic.

After 5 years, I left to spend more time with our teams in Charleston, South Carolina, and Sioux Falls, South Dakota.

I didn't leave because I was bored. The Saints had become icons. We were a fun, blue-collar alternative to the corporate Major League Baseball experience. We took chances, tweaked authority, and made fun of norms.

I left because I heard Dad in the back of my head. "McGill, know when to quit." Mom was the same way. She'd say, "Don't milk it, Milton," a reference to comedian Milton Berle, who would beat a joke to death until you couldn't stand it anymore.

I learned from Dad that people have shelf lives. He never stayed anywhere more than 5 or 6 years. Part of that was practical; he worked at such a frenetic pace that he needed to recharge his batteries every so often. Part of it was financial; he knew that the only way to make serious money in baseball was to sell the team. Part of it was philosophical; he always needed greater challenges.

Above all, he recognized that everyone needs a change of scenery. Had he stayed in Milwaukee or Cleveland his entire career, he probably would not have achieved such legendary status. He would never have been challenged to come up with the innovations and promotions he did, many of which were inspired by things unique to the various communities.

Perhaps his act would have worn thin after too many years in one place.

It's imperative that companies and individuals continually mix things up. It's the only way you stay fresh and keep improving. Even if you keep the same mix of people, rotate them to other departments. If your company has multiple branches or facets, keep people moving.

It keeps people on edge, forces them to develop new skills, and improves the company. By creating this natural anxiety and tension in a good way, it naturally helps the company redefine itself. It's always funny how the guy who ran the highly successful sales division for a decade seems irreplaceable until you bring in somebody else with new ideas. Meanwhile, the sales guy becomes even more valuable as your new director of business development. He's able to pursue ideas in other parts of the company he never could in sales.

Take someone in customer service and pay for him to take some accounting courses or pursue an MBA. Admittedly, some of these people might take these new skills and leave the company, but so what? It's just as likely they'll stay because they're fresh and most likely working in a new area.

Moving people around does not necessarily require geographic change. IBM became known as "I've Been Moved" and admittedly, this can be difficult on people. I moved 17 times the first 11 years of my life. Even now, I don't know where to call home. I'm footloose, but I recognize too that it's tough for some people to leave the only town they've known.

I once had an employee tell me he always had wanted to be the general manager of a team in a small midwestern town. When he got his wish, he found life unbearable away from the only city he'd ever known. Soon he was driving 4 hours "home" every weekend. Not long after that, we brought him back.

Still, I'd argue that geographic change is good. It keeps everyone fresh. The armed forces understand this. Even in peacetime, they move people around constantly. Granted, our country seems to be more homogenous all the time, with a Starbucks and a Subway on every corner, but you take something from each experience in a different city.

I love New York. Like Dad, I've always wanted to run the New York Yankees. That's the ultimate in our industry. But that center-of-the-universe mentality that pervades so much of New York business, especially the media field, is stifling. Everyone should spend a couple years of his or her life in New York, if only to get that perspective. The problem is that many New Yorkers have only that one perspective and assume that nothing else matters. The same is true of people who never leave small towns or any one city.

Some argue that there's no need to have change for the sake of change. I disagree. Sometimes you have to shake up the status quo. Maybe that seemingly indispensable person who has been doing the same thing for 29 years really is keeping the company from advancing.

If you're the chief running the company, don't be afraid to admit to employees that you've grown stale and need change. Even if you don't have the foggiest idea about how you're going to do it, keep preaching it. Ask for suggestions. Move people around. Solicit opinions. Hold the types of idea contests we discussed in Chapter 7.

That brings us to the individual and keeping the career fresh. Perhaps it sounds contradictory to hear that you need to constantly keep moving. After all, perhaps you've spent years trying to find that perfect Fun Is Good environment. But you need to keep pushing the creativity.

Ask yourself this: Do you have 10 years of experience, or 1 year repeated 10 times? People convince themselves that they're advancing because their titles change, when in reality the company has grown and the "senior" title reflects tenure more than advancement and growth.

One of the most abused elements of corporate life is the annual review. This should be a time for an employee to express where she would like to be in the next few years. In our organization, people write out their personal marketing plans for the next 3 to 5 years and share them with me—at least annually, but more often it's part of an ongoing dialogue.

An annual review really should be an annual *preview*. It might be the only time for an employee to lobby for change—or for the supervisor to realize that it's time for it. Most annual reviews tend to focus on the previous year, and the supervisor downplays or ignores accomplishments because she knows she can't offer more than the company-mandated 3 percent raise. The tone is tense, the employee is disgusted, and any potential for a productive chat on how this person can better contribute and grow is lost.

The tragedy is that the company never attempts to establish a personal relationship with the employee and never learns where this person can help. The employee should use it as motivation to seek out that nurturing, Fun Is Good environment elsewhere.

Corporate America frowns on ambition. Employees should be happy where they are, especially in a tough economy where health care benefits are being slashed and there's no such thing as long-term security. Just be happy your job isn't being outsourced to India, right?

Hogwash. You have every right to be ambitious, even within your current situation, and you should express it frequently— assuming, of course, that your work performance warrants increased responsibility.

It's incumbent upon supervisors to keep up with their employees on a personal level. As the landscape changes in your business, ask them what changes have occurred in their personal landscapes. A kid goes from right out of college to married with three kids 10 years later. She has different dreams. Maybe it's more money or a reassignment. You have to keep tabs on people.

That's especially difficult the more successful your company gets. If you're the one receiving the media attention and accolades, you become removed from what's important. Stop taking the bows, and get down there and find out what these people want to do. Do they want to be partners? Do they want to take your job?

We constantly move people up in our organization. Interns become staff members. Staff members become general managers. General managers become presidents and presidents become owners. We reward key people with an ownership slice in our ball clubs. There's no better motivator than giving people a piece of the action.

It's easy to sit back and figure these things will take care of themselves. The loyal employees will stay, and the malcontents will leave. The problem with this is that the malcontents often are the most valuable and have options. The loyal ones often are slugs who have nowhere else to go. Let this situation fester long enough and you're left with a company that no longer comes up with new ideas.

Never stop infusing a company with youth. That doesn't mean placing undue emphasis on 20-year-olds who have a skewed view of life, but there is something to be said for the energy level created by having young people in the office.

Wait, you say. We're a skilled business. You have to be at least 30 to work here. If that's the case, get some interns. It keeps you from getting stale.

It's amazing how quickly we lose touch. Disco Demolition reminded me how I had grown out of touch at the age of 28. When I said, "I hate disco," I meant let's bring back the Doors and Creedence Clearwater Revival. But the college kids who stormed the field that night didn't see it that way. They had missed the 1960s and viewed rebelling against disco as their cause, as if it were something significant.

Among the other thoughts that went through my mind as my career went up in a cloud of smoke over second base was how I had lost the pulse. I was a generation behind.

Youngsters are invaluable, and if you're too busy to invest some time in their future, you're cheating yourself. On days when I was running a club and the team was on the road, I would wait until 5:30 or 6 o'clock to see who was still in the office. The paycheck employees would already be gone, but inevitably I'd find some youngsters outside my office asking, "What else can we do?"

I knew instantly these were kids who were going to make it big.

Put kids to work on anything related to technology. People over the age of 30 understand the Internet and are quite proficient with all types of software. You have to be in order to compete in the twenty-first century. But it's second nature for anyone under 30. All of our Web designers are kids who have been doing such work since their teenage years.

Our scoreboard operator in Charleston, Lee Ziegler, is 12 years old. (I hope this doesn't get us in trouble with the labor board.) He's the best operator we've ever had because he grew up with a Gameboy in his hands and he loves baseball.

Put kids and young adults to work. You'll be amazed at the results.

As for the Saints, they thrived in the years after I departed. New people brought more ideas, and they managed to maintain and grow the Fun Is Good philosophy that had launched the company in 1993.

By 2003, it was time for another change. It had been 5 years since I left, and things had grown stale again. So we mixed things up, moved people around, and brought new ones in, ensuring that even an 11-year-old business could maintain the magic of opening day.

· ·

Fun Is Good Vignette

Jim "Mattress Mac" McIngvale, CEO of Gallery Furniture

"When you walk through our Gallery Furniture showroom in Houston, you never know what you're going to see. There's a huge Elvis Presley display, complete with his 1956 Mark II Lincoln Continental. There are jewels worn by Princess Diana, loads of sports memorabilia, and a 28-square-foot television tuned to major sporting events. We serve free hamburgers, hot dogs, and barbecue to customers every day."

You never know what promotion we'll have on tap. We treat every day as opening day in our store, which is the country's top revenue-producing, single-site retail operation, with sales of more than $150 million per year.

There are 300 outlets in Houston where people can buy furniture, but the reason they drive 60 miles past 15 other stores is that they're going to have fun when they get here. They can buy a sofa anywhere and the price won't be that different, but they buy from us because they like us, trust us, and believe in us—and they and their kids have fun when they're here.

You have to offer something more than furniture (or whatever product or service you have to offer). You have to get out of "commodity mode"; nobody makes money when all you do is sell a commodity. Turn your product into something bigger than what it is, which is what Mike Veeck does with minor league baseball. If he looked at baseball as just a commodity, he'd be no different than the dozens of other baseball teams and countless other entertainment options. Instead, he turns it into an incredible experience.

We recently had a mother come into the store with her twin 8-year-old boys. They had thrown tantrums when Mom told them they were going to spend a weekend afternoon furniture shopping. But by the time they left, they were asking when they could return because we had provided them with an amazing experience.

One of my mottos is "Always Think Big." It refers to this concept of making your business something greater than it is. The furniture store that we have might seem like just another furniture store to the everyday person, but to us it represents a dream of becoming the world's greatest retail store.

It started in 1981, when I started Gallery Furniture with just $5,000. I was—and remain—a tireless promoter. I starred in our TV commercials dressed up as a mattress. I figured if I wore a mattress, people would associate me with what I sell. So I started wearing a mattress, with holes for arms and legs and the head cut out. And I became known as "Mattress Mac."

Some people call our ads cheesy. Marketing students at the University of Houston put together a list of the worst ads each year, and we regularly top the list, but that's okay. We're not out to win any advertising awards. Our goal is to break through the clutter and make an impact. As long as the ads make customers laugh, we're doing something right.

We had a consultant analyze our business recently, and he asked if there was anything we did 10 years ago that we don't do now. I noticed that our ads were wackier back then. The TV spots have not gotten slick by any means, but they're not quite as irreverent as they were before.

We made it a point to dial it up a notch. It's easy to get conservative as your business matures, and you have to watch that. So I still put on the mattress suit occasionally. I'm not above doing that just because we've had some success. You have to continue to create that opening-day magic, and the only way to stay cutting edge is to continually change. If you don't change, you're not going to survive.

There's always some way to change. There are new ways to sell and market. You can enhance the customer experience. We used to have live bands in the store, but it got a little noisy. Still, it was worth trying.

Customer service is vital. You have to work on customers to earn their loyalty. We've become so spoiled in this country, obsessed with that instant gratification of what fun and thrill can I have today. So you have to provide a taste of that. Customers want to know what you've done for them in the last 15 minutes, and if you're not doing something that's personal, significant, and unexpected, they're going to go somewhere else.

You can never let up on customer service. Treat each customer as your first. You may have the greatest marketing and people may have a great time in the store, but if you screw up their delivery, you've failed. One bad cog in the experience ruins everything. If we drop the ball anywhere along the line, we've failed.

We believe in giving back to the community. We recently staged a health fair at our store to fight this huge national epidemic of obesity. We're always trying to do things that are good because it's part of the universal law of reciprocation. Do good things for people, and good things will happen to you.

Keep opening day alive. As our business became successful, I got involved in some other things. I purchased the struggling Westside Tennis Club and transformed it into a practice facility for the Houston Rockets basketball team. The facility has hosted major tennis events. Gallery Furniture sponsored a post-season college football game. We've promoted horse racing, championship wrestling, and even produced a Chuck Norris action movie called *Sidekicks*.

But I remain focused on Gallery Furniture. It remains a challenge to outfox competitors and to make people happy. Making people happy is the ultimate business; if we've done that, then we've accomplished something.

I'm more excited than ever about our business. There are so many more challenges and opportunities, and we never want to end up stagnant. We want to be growing and vibrant, and the only way to do that is to treat every day like opening day.

· ·

A Picnic at the Dump

One of the keys to keeping the magic of opening day alive is to constantly look at your business to see if you could do something differently.

When Dad ran the Chicago White Sox, he insisted that everyone, including himself, walk the ballpark constantly. Not just during games to solicit fan opinions and advice, but even when the team was out of town and during the off-season.

This inspired what perhaps is my greatest contribution to baseball: private fan picnic areas. I'm not looking to toot my own horn, but if I'm going to take the blame for the national plague of luxury suites and publicly financed sports venues, I'd like to offer this up as a modest defense.

Beginning with Dad's first stint as owner of the Chicago White Sox, fans could bring in food from the outside and picnic—for free—in an area behind left field. (These days, some baseball owners won't let fans bring in anything, not even bottled water.)

Not long after Dad reacquired the White Sox in 1975, we discovered an area near the entrance to the center field bleachers that was serving as a gigantic trash bin. The first thing Dad did upon taking over any operation was to clean up everything, but we decided to take it a step further by putting the space to use.

We painted, brought in picnic tables, and marketed the area to corporate groups that might want to have a meal together before the game. What once had been a stadium garbage dump became known as "the patio." Sounds simple now, but this didn't exist before the 1976 season. We were the first team to introduce the concept of a private party area.

This worked well as a pregame venue, but because you couldn't see the field, nobody wanted to sit there during games. We noticed that there were two unused bullpen areas underneath the stands that, for some reason, had been enclosed.

We called a press conference and with great fanfare, Dad took a sledgehammer to the walls that blocked the view of the field from the bullpen. Suddenly we had private party areas with a view of the game. This joined the original picnic area in left field, which, of course, was still free. Along with my inaugural skybox, we had five private areas to market to groups, which was important. Back then we needed every dime just to remain solvent.

These days, nearly every baseball team in the majors and minors has some sort of pregame or in-game picnic area. If we had not come up with the concept, someone else would have eventually. But it's an example of how you can take any element of your business—even a dumpy storage area used for garbage—and use it to re-create the magic of opening day.

● ●

FUN IS GOOD

Chapter 9 Summary and Exercises (Every Day Is Opening Day)

- Change is good.
- Do you have 10 years of experience, or 1 year repeated 10 times? How can you implement change in your career to become more productive and happier?
- Companies not constantly evolving become stale. Implement change to prevent a downturn, not in response to one.
- Move employees around: to other departments, and even around the country. If you're the chief, this includes you. It keeps workers and the company fresh.
- Craft a 3-year and a 5-year marketing plan for yourself. Review and revise it regularly.
- Make ownership stakes in the company available to key employees, no matter how small and how private your company.
- Know when to leave. Greater challenges are out there.

Chapter 10

Customer Service

Once the Fun Is Good philosophy is instilled in your organization, you'll have upbeat, motivated employees who will provide superior customer service. As an employee, you'll enjoy your job more if you feel like you're helping others have fun.

Customer service should not be a department but the underlying theme of your company. Everyone should be committed to and actively involved in providing superior customer service. Every element of Fun Is Good relates to customer service. This is where passion, attitude, ideas, irreverence, chiefs and Indians, the human touch, laughter, and everything Bill Veeck stood for come together.

Customer service is a dying art in our country. Show me a successful company, and I'll show you one that provides excellent customer service. Though there are many reasons why a company fails, a lack of customer service is often the leading culprit.

Take Southwest Airlines (which I actually do on a fairly regular basis when I travel). In recent years, Southwest has been among the few profitable airlines. Much of its success is because of its sound business model. Southwest avoids the crowded hub system, takes advantage of underused airports, turns its flights around quickly, and, of course, offers low, low fares.

But much of Southwest's popularity and success stems from its customer service. Its employees are unfailingly cheerful, especially the captains and flight attendants who crack jokes and make flying fun. Rarely does anyone get off a plane smiling these days, but that often happens when you fly Southwest. The company even sends its frequent flyer customers birthday cards—"It seems like only yesterday you walked down the aisle"—and makes an effort to personalize service.

Southwest's check-in lines are usually short, and it's possible to get through on the phone to a live person quickly, unlike other airlines that make it difficult to reach anyone within 10 minutes.

Travelers have no patience for excuses and inconveniences. The airline that provides the best customer service receives their business. Because Southwest gets Fun Is Good, it provides superior customer service and thus runs the most profitable U.S. airline. Midwest Express Airlines, though perhaps not as irreverent as Southwest, also is known for its commitment to customer service and, not surprisingly, is one of the nation's most successful airlines. It's no wonder that airlines such as JetBlue and Delta's new Song Airlines have modeled themselves after Southwest and Midwest Express.

Several years ago, Leonard L. Berry wrote a best-selling book called *Discovering the Soul of Service: The 9 Drivers of Sustainable Business Success,* in which he cited 14 companies, including Midwest Express, Charles Schwab, and our St. Paul Saints, as the nation's best companies at emphasizing "values-driven leadership, generosity, and investment success to help deliver customer satisfaction, innovation, and growth."

That all sounds very impressive, and we're very proud of our rating from Mr. Berry, but when you boil it down, it comes down to customer service. Now, every company *says* they strive to provide wonderful customer service, but how many actually do?

. . . .

The Wait Is the Hardest Part . . . But Easy to Fix

I'm not going to name names, but there are a number of chain restaurants that have no clue about customer service. They serve pretty much the same menu—grilled chicken, club sandwiches, fajitas, wings, steak, fish, perhaps Italian food—and have the same basic decor, with a bar in the middle or out front, and perhaps some tin reproductions of vintage advertising on the walls.

If you walk into one of these establishments at dinnertime, you'll often be told there's a 30-minute wait, even though half the restaurant is empty. So, you're given one of those vibrating coasters and sent to the bar, where you begrudgingly order some overpriced drinks while waiting for a table to "open."

These restaurants spend millions marketing their fun, family atmosphere—and indeed there's truth in their advertising. But that goodwill is canceled out when you walk into one of these half-empty places and are told to wait. It's annoying. Perhaps you leave and go somewhere else.

What's even more frustrating is to request to sit in a quiet area so you can discuss business with your companions only to be told the section is closed.

I know restaurant gurus will say it's more profitable to have people in the bar and keep traffic moving at a furious pace through one-half or three-quarters of the restaurant rather than having a slower pace with the entire place open.

That works for the short term. But what happens when people are fed up with waiting for a seat at your half-empty restaurant? As the great philosopher Yogi Berra once said, "The place is so busy, nobody goes there anymore."

These restaurants have created superficial waiting time because they don't want to open another section or put two more employees on the shift. Instead of asking why they don't have enough customers to keep the entire restaurant busy and then doing something about it, they concede business and alienate the remaining diners who have to wait.

Major League Baseball does this occasionally, closing off the upper decks of ballparks. They tore down a generation of 65,000-seat venues, in part because they were antiquated, but also because they gave up trying to fill them. Instead, they built replicas of the 42,000-seat ballparks of the 1950s that were demolished back when demand started to exceed the supply of tickets. Then they pat themselves on the back for filling these smaller venues, though these days even a new ballpark is no guarantee of increased demand.

Following that progression, I expect fern bar restaurants to get smaller in the coming years as customers get frustrated with the wait.

Businesses need to be respectful of their customers' time. Some people like to have a 3-hour dining experience, but most others would like to have a decent meal that doesn't involve fast food in an hour or less. Given that fern bar food is pretty much the same, customer service will determine who gets the business.

In our ballparks, we've found that keeping all of the concession stands open regardless of the size of the crowd is good business. People will buy more of your product and come back if they don't have to wait.

· ·

To give quality customer service, you have to be able to deal with complaints. The complaint is the greatest power a customer has. You know how it is when you call someone to complain. Someone picks up the phone, listens for a brief moment, and then places you on hold while they figure out how to get rid of you. While you're on hold, everyone in the office has their heads buried in cubicles. No one wants to deal with you.

I've found the best way to deal with complaints is to meet them head-on. After nearly 20 years of being out of Major League Baseball, I got a chance to become the senior vice president of sales and marketing for the Tampa Bay Devil Rays. For our first game of the 1999 season, we drew more than 40,000 fans. I was thrilled. So thrilled, in fact, that I decided to shoot off some fireworks during the national anthem. The only problem was that the Devil Rays play in an indoor stadium. The smoke lingered throughout the game and, sure enough, late in the contest Rays' outfielder Randy Winn lost a ball in the smoke, leading to a run for the other team.

The day after Winn lost the ball, we received dozens of calls, wanting to know how we could be so stupid as to set off indoor fireworks. A few cheap theatrics could have cost the team the game. (In fact, the Rays lost, 4 to 1.) Fans were livid. Whose side was I on?

I'd pick up the phone and the first thing I'd hear was "I want to talk to that moron Mike Veeck."

"You've got him," I'd say. "Look, I know I'm a moron. That was a boneheaded thing to do."

That's all it took to disarm the callers. Most of the time, people just want to vent. But those complaints, the phone calls that none of us want to take, are the best source of information we can receive as businesspeople. Instead of having a so-called complaint department, we should all be our own complaint department and take the calls ourselves.

You know what really gets people mad? It's not whatever you've done to tick them off to the point of calling you. It's when they do call you and they get an automated system that tells them to "press 1 if you'd like to speak to so-and-so."

Voice mail is infuriating. How about just picking up the phone and saying, "Hello, can I do something for you?" Isn't that what being in business is all about? One of the first things I learned from my dad was: Pick up your own phone.

When Dad ran the St. Louis Browns (now the Baltimore Orioles), the team rarely drew any fans, and Dad, in a warped sort of way, thrived on that. He'd walk through the grandstands talking to the 11 or 12 customers he had. He was the owner and general manager, sold tickets and soda, and did whatever needed to be done. He provided superior customer service himself because he couldn't afford to hire too much help. But that kind of personal attention attracted repeat customers.

My dad was ubiquitous, another key element of customer service. Be everywhere. Take the calls. Handle the complaints yourself. Be self-deprecating, and don't take yourself too seriously.

One day, my dad picked up the phone, and a woman from out of town was on the line. "I want to buy a dozen tickets to see the St. Louis Browns," she said.

My father nearly fell out of his chair. "Yes, ma'am," he said, composing himself.

"What time does the game start?" she asked.

"What time is convenient for you to be here?"

"Now don't you get smart with me, young man," she said. "I want the best seats in the house."

"How about second base?" my dad said. "We haven't used that all year."

Your customers will tell you about your product. The worst thing about the way American businesses are set up is that the farther up the ladder you go, the farther away you are from your customer. It shouldn't be that way. I'm fortunate to have actor Bill Murray among my business partners. He owns pieces of these minor league baseball teams with me. And in places like St. Paul; Charleston, South Carolina; Hudson Valley, New York; and Brockton, Massachusetts; he'll sometimes be out there in front of the gate taking your ticket or sitting in the stands signing autographs.

People sometimes accuse us of using Bill as a photo opportunity, but that's not quite fair. We do it because there's no better place to learn about our fans and what they like about our product than in front of the stadium. You can't sit in a luxury owner's suite at the ballpark—or in your cushy executive office in some glass tower—and expect to have your finger on the pulse of your customers. You have to be at the entry gate, out on the front lines, in the stores, at the trade shows talking to the people that ultimately determine the success of your business.

Customer service requires super vision. You'll note that I use super *vision,* not supervision. There's a huge difference. I believe that most employees want to see a super vision. They want to believe that there is a great plan for 3 to 5 years out, and they don't want to think that their supervisors are going to be constantly looking over their shoulders trying to ascertain whether they have a clue. We have to let our employees do their jobs. Open your ears to everyone in your organization, and you'll find that ideas flow freely.

And when those ideas start coming, it's up to you to try them. When I was with the Devil Rays, a group of marketing guys asked me what sort of promotion we would have for Labor Day.

"We'll let all of the pregnant women in for free," I said.

I thought this was pretty funny. But no one was laughing. The guy who asked the question looked particularly puzzled. "Well, um, how are we going to know?"

"They have baby detection devices," I said.

All I got was another blank look. I think the guy thought I was serious.

They held Labor Day at Tropicana Field that year, 3 months after I left, but like my "pinball baseball," it ended up watered down and forgettable. One of my fellow minor league owners took the idea and ran with it and generated tons of media coverage. He not only let all of the pregnant women in free but also promised to give a year's supply of diapers to the first woman who gave birth during the game. He gave away baby furniture, toys, bottles, and all of the things that cost new parents a fortune.

Look, we live in a society that has lost its sense of humor. We need to try things, to make fun of things. The marketing guys with the Devil Rays meant well, but the first thing that came to their minds was the logistics of it all and how it might be perceived. We've become far too uptight.

So try new ideas in the workplace. As Chris Sullivan says, there are no rules. Outback Steakhouse has done pretty well with that philosophy. Remember, customers prefer to deal with companies that take chances. I can ask a room full of businesspeople what they think about change, and everyone will say, "Change is great. We love change. Change is our livelihood." But although 80 percent of the companies in this country pay lip service to loving change, only 20 percent of that 80 percent actually change. We're creatures of habit, and change is very frightening.

Always ask yourself what the customer wants. Do research. Ask your customers questions. They love to talk about themselves. Get them on the phone. Remember the customer who calls to complain? The longer you can talk to that person, the more you will learn.

Research gets a bad rap. If you walk into your office and announce to your staff that you're going to do some research, everyone will groan. But if you look at it as nothing more than daily interaction with customers, it will not only be fun but also pay handsome dividends.

It's amazing the ideas a little customer research can produce. One season, my dad began to notice that there were more women at the ballpark. Since any spike in attendance was cause for rejoicing, my dad wanted to make sure he maintained this good fortune. So he began talking to our female fans, asking them what they liked and didn't like about coming to the ballpark.

One woman said she didn't know any of the players. Dad asked her what he should do. She suggested that he put the names on the backs of uniforms. Today, most every team throughout sports has names on the backs of uniforms, all because of the informal research my dad conducted.

It's simple, really. Ask people what they want and they will tell you. Remember: They know your business better than you do.

Sometimes the best ideas come to you over the phone, which is yet another reason not to screen your calls. When we were getting ready for the inaugural season of the St. Paul Saints, I got a call from a woman who said she was a Roman Catholic nun who gave massages. I wanted to hang up. Even I wanted no part of that potential can of worms.

She was persistent. "Look, I know you're starting a ball club in Minnesota. I'm a businesswoman in St. Paul. I'm a Roman Catholic nun and I give massages. I'm telling you the truth."

Not only was she telling the truth, but she was a smash hit at St. Paul Saints games. Now Sister Rosalind Gefre has become much more than an institution in Minnesota. These days, she gives massages at Minnesota Vikings and Timberwolves games.

None of it would have happened if I had been screening my calls. The greatest people will walk right through your door if you're receptive and you just answer the phone. Plus, it's fun. Maybe one time you'll pick up the phone and it will be that relative you can't stand, but another time it will be someone wonderful.

People know when their calls are being screened. Believe me, I know. Do you think anyone takes *my* calls? I have to make up names.

Don't screen your calls.

Out in the office, encourage your employees. We live in a time when people need the human touch. We worry about things like technology when what we should really be worrying about is how we've become so desensitized that we have to weigh our words before we give someone a compliment. Why don't we take the time to encourage one another and give everyone the kind of support they need?

Customer service requires responsiveness. You have to be responsive to your customers. We thought we'd have 3,000 people show up at our first game in St. Paul. Instead, we had 6,000. When you're dealing with a lack of portable toilets, as we were that evening, you can imagine the problems we soon had. The lines were long and the stench was terrible. So Bill Murray, who was on hand that evening, went out and bought a ton of incense. Then he went into every Port-a-John and burned it.

Granted, the resulting stench might have been even worse, but the fact that Bill Murray took the time to attempt customer service made it newsworthy. The bottom line was we responded—and responded quickly.

Several years ago, a guy from a major news magazine came to St. Paul to do a story on the Saints. He was there the night we had a Bob Dylan concert. Afterward, the reporter was interviewing me up in the grandstands. He was a cocky Hollywood type, and he asked me where he might find Bill Murray.

"Down there," I said, pointing to the base of the stage. "He's the guy out there with my wife picking up cigarette butts."

"Yeah, right," the guy said. "C'mon, where's Bill Murray?"

Now there isn't a single job that any of the employees in our six minor league baseball organizations will not do because they've seen and picked up trash alongside Bill Murray. We all need to be willing to do things in the workplace that we'd ask others to do. We should be responsive and receptive, not only for our customers but also the people with whom we work.

• •

Costco

When I think of companies that embody the Fun Is Good concept of providing superior customer service and showing a genuine interest in their employees, I think of Costco Wholesale, those big-box shopping outlets where you can buy everything from milk and gas to clothes, jewelry, and big-screen TVs.

Here's a company that does everything Wall Street hates. It provides its employees with among the highest wages and best benefits in retail, which creates loyalty. It caps its markup on products at 14 percent, miniscule for retail, and that creates customer loyalty. Costco charges $45 a year for membership but has a staggering renewal rate of 86 percent. It lets customers return merchandise with no receipts and no questions asked—with virtually no time limits.

Costco's CEO, Jim Sinegal, caps his salary at $350,000 and rarely takes a bonus. Granted, he owns a lot of stock, but most Fortune 500 CEOs would shudder at the thought of such a low salary.

The company operates under two simple rules: Take care of your customer, and take care of your employees.

Walk into a Costco and you'll find people providing customer service with a smile. Because there's a low rate of employee turnover, you might actually get to know some of them, just as it was decades ago when you might develop a rapport with the butcher or stock boy. Employees take the time to interact and get to know your kids.

Shopping at Costco is fun because it deals in high-end merchandise and rotates some of its stock continuously. You never know what you might find. Perhaps oak armoires one week, leather jackets the next.

You can find almost anything at Costco, including liquor, office supplies, tires, film processing, flowers, and groceries, but what separates the company from Sam's Club and other wholesale outlets is its dedication to the employee and customer. Nobody else can touch Costco in that department.

Costco has far fewer stores than Sam's but has higher sales. Profits might be lower, but the Wal-Mart empire doesn't cater to the employee and customer the way Costco does.

Wall Street loves companies like Wal-Mart, of course. Listen to Deutsche Bank analyst Bill Dreher, quoted in *Fortune* magazine: "Costco continues to be a company that is better at serving the club member and employee than the shareholder."

Heaven forbid!

I imagine that Dreher is among the Wall Street types banging the drum for Costco to cut benefits and jack up prices. That's typical short-term thinking.

Look at any consumer category and you'll find the long-term leaders are not just those with great products but with superior customer service. Do you think Ritz-Carlton and the Four Seasons could command such staggering room rates were it not for their can-do reputations for customer service? Do you think an airline like Southwest, with its no-frills service, would be so successful were it not for its fun, customer-friendly reputation?

How about Nordstrom's? Sure, they sell some great merchandise. But this company, which has outlasted so many other similar upscale retailers, thrives because its calling card is unsurpassed customer service.

Maybe Wall Street doesn't like Costco. Who cares? If I'm a customer or employee, I love the company.

"We think when you take care of your customer and your employees, your shareholders are going to be rewarded in the long run," Sinegal told *Fortune*. "And I'm one of them [the shareholders]; I care about the stock price. But we're not going to do something for the sake of one quarter that's going to destroy the fabric of our company and what we stand for."

Let the Wall Street cynics snicker. The companies that will survive over the next decade are the ones that treat employees well and provide superior customer service.

Without that, your company is just a big box without a soul.

• •

If we can do that, then customer service will start to provide *value*. When you arrive at a Four Seasons hotel, they know what you want. It's there on the computer. They know all of your preferences, including the fact that you require a nonsmoking room with two double beds on an upper floor. When you arrive at a nice restaurant, you want to be greeted by name and seated at whatever table you like for whatever reason.

No matter what your business, you should strive to provide that kind of value. I know I can't just sell baseball tickets. It has to be an event; it can't be just a game. I have to make sure that every 8-year-old boy or girl at the ballpark feels like he or she is the most important person in the world.

Customer service requires extra effort. I always carry stacks of postcards. Whenever I finish a meeting with a client, I send a hand-written postcard immediately. I thank that person for taking time out to see me. Each year, I send a handwritten postcard to every season ticket holder in St. Paul. That's roughly 1,000 postcards. It takes a while, but it makes a difference. The Saints have a renewal rate of better than 90 percent for season tickets, which is well above the average in sports.

Our staff does a tremendous job catering to the customer and providing a Fun Is Good experience every night, but I reinforce this spirit of appreciation each winter when I write a personal note to every season ticket holder thanking them for their patronage.

Granted, we don't have 40,000 season ticket holders like your average NFL franchise, but writing 1,000 or so brief messages on postcards still takes some time and effort. I have them preaddressed and stamped and work on them while on planes, waiting in line, and whenever I have a spare moment. Thankfully, our capable staff affords me such time.

When I first started writing the notes, people couldn't believe it. They smudged the ink just to make sure it wasn't preprinted.

When was the last time you handwrote a thank-you card to one of your customers? You'd be amazed at how that breeds customer loyalty.

But it's more than just postcards. I make it a point to call my important clients on Saturday or Sunday or in the evening to let them know that we're thinking about their business all the time. I love to get a call from my ad agency at 9 p.m. from the account representative saying she has a great idea.

As we move further into the new millennium, service will determine success. People will expect products to be great. The difference will be the people who service them and the people who sell those products. Companies often make the mistake of putting the so-called talented people in sales and marketing and sticking whomever in customer service. But that department is the one that will determine the public perception of your company. Without quality customer service, your company is destined to fail.

No matter where you stand in the corporate food chain, apply the Fun Is Good philosophy. If you can adapt this sense of irreverence and caring in your workplace, if you can take your job but not yourself seriously, then providing this customer service will be effortless.

. . . .

Dealing with Mail

The next time you're on eBay, do a search for "Bill Veeck." Chances are you'll come up with someone looking to sell a personalized letter they received from Dad.

These notes don't sell for as much as you'd expect, considering Dad hasn't been writing letters for nearly 20 years. I know Dad would be proud of the market for his handwritten notes. Not because he would object to someone making money off his name—heck, several people have auctioned his peg legs—but because he would be glad that supply far outweighs demand.

Since he wrote so many, Bill Veeck letters are not very rare. Unfortunately, it's almost unheard of for people to write personal notes these days.

That's a shame because there's nothing quite as effective as a personal note. Not a personal e-mail, though that's better than nothing, but a personal note. Everyone should get in the habit of writing letters in their personal and professional lives.

People hate form letters. Some companies think that substituting the individual's name and address instead of writing "Dear Occupant/Customer" makes a difference, but people can see right through it. A personal touch makes a difference, now more than ever.

Customers want more than quality products. They want to be appreciated. Short personalized notes like the ones I send to the St. Paul Saints season ticket holders make all the difference.

I can't stand form letters and anything that reeks of mass distribution. I credit my parents for that. Long before it became trendy, they would take the postage-paid envelopes out of junk mail and send them back empty. Sometimes they'd swap the junk mail and send it back (removing all traces of identification, of course).

I recommend you do the same. By sending back envelopes empty, you're fining companies for that lack of personalized service and for cluttering your mailbox. You're also supporting the United States Postal Service, which helps the economy.

I recently struck up a conversation on an airplane with a gentleman who works for Nextel, the cellular phone company. We exchanged business cards, and I followed up with a handwritten note.

I forwarded his information to Liz Adams, one of our salespeople in St. Paul, and she ended up selling him a $35,000 sponsorship package. He told her he was floored that someone still would take the time to send a personalized note.

Try the personal touch. Instead of a form letter or a perfunctory e-mail, send back a handwritten letter. You'll be amazed at the results.

• •

FUN IS GOOD

Chapter 10 Summary and Exercises (Customer Service)

- Customer service is just as important as product and price in separating successful companies from unsuccessful ones.
- Pick up the phone. Deal with complaints head-on. Let customers vent.
- Owners and executives need to work the front lines of customer service.
- List five things you can do to better serve the customer.
- Make customers laugh. Fun companies attract loyal customers and talented employees.
- Listen to customers. They know your business best and will give you great ideas.
- Every customer should feel like he or she is the most important person in the world.
- Eliminate customer waiting whenever possible.
- Make the extra effort: Send handwritten thank-you notes.

Chapter 11

Giving Back

Once you've benefited from Fun Is Good, it's time to give something back. Call it karma, reaping what you sow, or the right thing to do. Whatever you call it, you'll feel good about it.

Giving back takes two primary forms: sharing knowledge with others through mentoring, and giving to the community through volunteer work.

I learned from Dad that mentoring and volunteering not only are the right things to do, but they're also good for business. If you give your time, talent, and money to charity, you're going to foster tremendous goodwill in your community. If you pass on your knowledge to young employees, you're going to make your life easier.

In both instances, you'll get back far more than you put in—and even if you can't quantify it, you'll reap the intangible rewards of helping others.

Let's start with volunteering. There's nothing that fosters a better sense of perspective; it gives you an appreciation for what you have. I have a dear friend who has been out of work for a couple of years. He's going through personal bankruptcy; it's the worst time of his life. Except for a few breaks along the way, I could have been that guy, and that's what volunteering and giving back means. We've all had some people help us along the way, and it's incumbent upon us to give it back.

The movie *Pay It Forward* portrayed this concept perfectly. People performed random acts of generosity in response to something that had happened to them. I'm obviously going to do everything I can to help my buddy who is down on his luck, but giving back is more about doing things for people you don't know.

Volunteerism and charitable giving is soaring because people have discovered that racking up material possessions and professional accomplishments isn't as fulfilling as helping others. As we discussed earlier, it's important to remove the self-centeredness from your world.

You need not have specific talents to volunteer. Anyone can read to kids or deliver Meals on Wheels, as my wife, Libby, does. She looks forward to her route each week. Anyone can paint houses, perform odd jobs, or visit nursing homes.

If you run a company, give employees time off to volunteer. Employees who are given one afternoon a week to read to kids or mentor young people are going to be so much more productive because they'll have a better appreciation for their life situations. It will also make them less likely to participate in that popular corporate pastime: whining.

If your company can provide this opportunity, your employees will benefit from this emotional fulfillment. Not only that, there's tremendous reward externally from being regarded as a civic-minded company.

It's more than just joining a chamber of commerce, sponsoring a Little League team, or getting involved in something like Habitat for Humanity—all worthy causes.

What if you shut down your company for a day and put all of your employees to work in the community? That's an awful lot of man-hours to unleash upon your town. You could issue a press release or take out an ad in the paper to let everyone know, not because it's self-serving but because you want the community to help your employees make the most of that opportunity. Not only that, but you can take the opportunity to be irreverent. Announce that everyone is playing hooky for a day.

Whether you volunteer on an individual level or because your company affords you regular time or sponsors a daylong affair, the rewards are huge. Obviously, it's the right thing to do and employees will be more productive, but the community will see your company's commitment and be more likely to support your business.

We see this all the time in minor league baseball. Because our employees take an active role in the community, people view us as something of a civic treasure. That's not as easy as it sounds, even at the minor league level, where jaded sports fans increasingly view sports operations as stripping every dollar possible out of a community without giving anything back.

Yet sponsors and advertisers tell us all the time that the reason they support us is that they view us as a way of supporting the community. That's kind of a backhanded compliment since we like to think we provide effective sponsor and advertising value, but if we've added a few marketing partners as a result of our volunteering, that's wonderful.

Volunteer. If you're in position to encourage volunteering, do so. The upside is tremendous.

Now that you've given back externally through volunteering, take a look inside your company.

Aside from parenting, there's no more valuable role you can play than being a mentor. Take a rising star in your organization, someone who has a genuine interest in learning, and show that person the ropes. Give them the tools to succeed.

I worked alongside my father for 6 years, and I learned a lot through osmosis, but he wasn't my mentor. Rudie Schaffer, who served as the general manager of my dad's various businesses for 45 years, took the time to show me how things were done. He was patient enough to let me make mistakes and firm enough to get on my case when I wasn't paying attention or applying myself enough.

Mentoring is the greatest gift you can give someone. In Rudie's case, it was as much a gift to my dad as to me, but that's beside the point. Rudie was a talented teacher, and that's what we need more of in the workplace. Instead of worrying that youngsters are going to take your job, show them how to do it. The only immortality we have is whether we've affected people, not only in the workplace but in life. Rudie is retired now, but many of us who worked for him call ourselves "Rudie's Rascals."

We've always valued mentoring in the Goldklang Group, but this philosophy came into focus for me after my daughter, Rebecca, was diagnosed with retinitis pigmentosa. I realized that there is a whole world of people dealing with similar situations, maybe not retinitis pigmentosa specifically, but other equally horrible ailments. Everyone needs help with something.

It's the same thing in the workplace. There are people out there who can help you, but everyone is afraid to ask. Nobody wants to come across as vulnerable.

Be that person who offers to be a mentor. It's not a formal process where you meet with a young protégé and announce, "Today, we are embarking on a mentor relationship."

It's more subtle than that. As a mentor, you need to give these people plum assignments and the chance to fail. Work them harder than anyone else so others in the office don't look at them as the teacher's pet. Challenge them and try to break them to make sure that your instincts about their potential are correct.

Give these upstarts the freedom to come after you, to ask pointed questions, and to challenge you. Allow them some leeway that others don't have, just as long as it remains a private one-on-one relationship. You don't want them challenging you publicly.

Soon you'll find that these people rise to the top. They come early, stay late, and deliver more results than others. Sometimes you provide the opportunity and it ends up being a waste of time when the person doesn't respond. But that's okay. Companies stop growing when they give up on the process.

I constantly remind managers in our organization to find their next star. You should be training somebody to take your job. This isn't just altruistic because there's a lot in it for you and your company.

After all, if you can train people to do your job, it buys you the freedom to do other things, to focus on special projects and the elements of your role you enjoy most. The end result is a lot more freedom for you and others throughout the company because you've mentored these people to take charge and handle things on their own.

If you're someone searching for a mentor, look for the person who represents what you want to be. Express admiration for how that person performs the job and ask if you can help with a project. Mention that you have something to bring to the table and would like to help but just need an opening.

For some reason, women are more apt to do this. They'll walk into my office, close the door, and say, "That guy down the hall? I want to know what he knows." Some approach a potential mentor directly.

If you're high up in the organization, you should be mentoring someone and also matching people up in mentor relationships. People don't realize how valuable it is to handle people this way. You're like an air traffic controller, pointing folks in the right directions.

Guys generally won't be forward in seeking mentor relationships; they view it as a sign of weakness. But you have to seek out mentors in order to succeed. Sometimes it's as simple as asking to be part of a project or emulating that person. If she stays late, you stay late. Inevitably, it will lead to a conversation. You can break the ice by complimenting them on a recent project or campaign.

Interns often get the benefit of the mentoring relationship—or at least they should. Too many companies use interns to perform menial tasks, and many never get beyond the coffee-and-copies stage. That's not always the company's fault. Interning is a two-way street, and it's incumbent upon the intern to seek out mentors and additional challenges.

I've never understood why companies don't use interns more. Here you have a group of hard-charging, enthusiastic young people who want nothing more than to learn everything they can from you, prove that they can cut it in your business, and do it all for college credit or a modest stipend. What do you have to lose?

Nobody is a bigger fan of interns than I am because I've seen the results. Not only do some of them become your best employees, but they're also fiercely loyal because of that initial opportunity. We have a young man in our organization, Derek Sharrer, who started as an intern 12 years ago, worked in various capacities for our teams, and now is general manager of our team in St. Paul. Derek no doubt could move on to other things, and perhaps one day he will, but we're tickled that he's remained with us.

I cringe whenever I hear of a company that's cut back on its intern program. Why? Usually you're not paying them anything. I quit my job as senior vice president for the Detroit Tigers in part because they were threatening to get rid of their intern program in Lakeland, Florida, home of their spring training headquarters and one of their minor league affiliates.

This news came up during a conference call of executives. My frustration with the Tigers had been building for some time. As with the Devil Rays and Marlins, the Tigers were struggling to buy into Fun Is Good. When they said they were cutting the intern program, I'd had enough. I said that if they really wanted to save some money, they needed to get rid of some vice presidents. I said I'd solve the problem right then and quit.

After I hung up, there was a pause. "He's kidding, right?" someone asked.

No, I was very serious.

Many companies miss a wonderful opportunity to mentor these young people, some of whom could become valuable full-time employees. They can learn much about your business at little or no salary and step right into a prominent role. But the reason this does not occur in many workplaces is that the intern selection process is flawed. You end up taking on the children of friends and you end up babysitting someone who really doesn't want to be there.

Sometimes the children of friends turn out to be effective interns. As someone who had to overcome the label of being the son of the boss, I'm sensitive to this. I've also found that those interns who arrive through a connection instead of by fiercely lobbying for the opportunity usually don't work out, especially in our business where they're working 15-hour days during baseball season.

I tell interns that they're going to have to work harder than they ever have before. Like all of our employees, they'll be expected to do everything, no matter how unglamorous the task. If they can survive the long hours and do a good job, I'll place them in a full-time gig with one of our teams.

Another problem with intern selection is that it's often done by the human resources department. Since HR departments rarely have an understanding of what an intern is going to do, they rarely come up with qualified candidates.

Take ownership of the intern selection process. Many of our interns made their initial contact by introducing themselves to me after a speech, and we've gotten some talented people this way. I've developed a sixth sense about this, to the point where I can see a sparkle in their eyes and just know.

I care much more about cover letters than résumés, and this applies to interns and new employees. Cover letters provide many signposts. You weed out the ones where they don't get your name right—that happens a lot with Veeck—and are poorly written and sloppy.

Bad grammar, spelling, and punctuation are signs of someone who doesn't read, and that's a big strike in our organization, where we value well-rounded people and those who can write and communicate well. We also hear from a lot of people with sports marketing degrees who figure they'll fit right in with our organization because, well, we engage in sports marketing. It's the same with any company. There's no passion in the letter, just a fill-in-the-blanks request.

"I recently obtained an accounting degree from State U. and would like to apply my skills to your fine accounting firm." Or this:

"I need an internship to fulfill my degree and given your proximity to my school, I thought I might be a good fit."

Ugh. Show some passion. There are people out there more than willing to give you a chance, but meet us halfway. I'd rather see people who are rabid about wanting to work for my organization. The best ones are those who approach either in person or in writing and say, "I want to do what you do."

. . . .

Fun Is Good Vignette

Dave Dombrowski,
President and CEO Detroit Tigers

"I had a wonderful mentor in Roland Hemond, who, during my early days with the Chicago White Sox at the age of 21, told me that I could feel free to ask him any question at any time."

"I've been doing this for a long time," he said. "I'm willing to help in any way possible. It's not going to affect my job situation. So let me know what you need."

Back in those days, the 1970s, Bill Veeck owned the White Sox. Mike Veeck worked in the front office, which by the standards of modern big league baseball employed precious few people.

Roland, the team's general manager, made it a point to send me out on the road to spend time with our scouts and player development staffs. He made sure I had every opportunity to immerse myself in the game, and his mentoring was a main reason I became, in 1988, the youngest (at 32) general manager in baseball history, to that point.

With such a small staff in Chicago, it was natural that I seek out Roland. These days, big-league baseball teams, like many corporations, are larger and it's not always obvious where to find that mentor relationship.

A lot of people actively seek out a mentor, someone who can help them grow, and that's a good thing. But more often than not, it just happens. If you work as hard as you can and pay attention to the task at hand, chances are someone will take you under his or her wing.

The key is to do your job so efficiently that you'll be available to pitch in when a potential mentor needs something. If you've taken care of your immediate responsibilities, then you can jump in with a positive attitude. If you haven't, then your immediate supervisor is more likely to mention that you're not meeting requirements as it is. You don't want to lose that opportunity.

Of course, you need to have a burning passion for this to work. A mentor doesn't want to waste time with someone who isn't truly interested.

I often hear from people who want to work in baseball. I remind them that I made just $8,000 a year when I got into the game, after negotiating with Mike up from $7,000. Even now, though I'm handsomely compensated, I'm working or on call every day of the year. Don't get me wrong; I'm happy the way things are. But I could not have been as successful in other fields as I've been in baseball because I did not have that passion.

Without that passion, I could not have convinced Roland and Mike to hire me, let alone have Roland as my mentor.

So find that passion first. Once you've identified it and entered your chosen profession, do your job so well that the mentor relationship will become a natural evolution.

Eventually, you'll be in a position to mentor someone. If you can identify that passion in others, you'll have no problem picking out those to mentor. Start by letting them get their feet wet, and gradually give them greater exposure and responsibility. In the short term, that frees you up to focus on what most needs your attention.

At some point, others will want to hire them. Perhaps they can take your job, allowing you to advance. I was able to move up from general manager to president and CEO because for years I had such capable assistant general managers that they allowed me to branch out into other areas of running a baseball business.

Being a mentor is tremendously rewarding, and I daresay that behind any successful person is a mentor whose wisdom is being passed down to a new generation of passionate people.

FUN IS GOOD

Chapter 11 Summary and Exercises (Giving Back)

- Volunteer work is not just personally rewarding, but it's also good for business.
- Give employees time off for volunteer work.
- Companies need to take an active role in their communities.
- Find someone to mentor. You should be training the next star of your company.
- If you're a younger employee, seek out a mentor. Look for someone who represents what you want to be.
- Interns are a valuable commodity. Teach them and let them help you.
- What three things could you assign interns that would make your life easier *and* benefit their development? If you are an intern, what three things could you do that would fit this description?
- Train someone to take your job. Make yourself indispensable by developing talent.

Chapter 12

Through the Eyes of a Child

Every day I wake up, and the first thing I think of is my daughter, Rebecca. She's been the leading inspiration in my life, especially after that terrible day in 1998. I thought I would have to teach her how to deal with this tragedy. As it turns out, I've been the one learning.

At the age of 7, Rebecca was diagnosed with a form of retinitis pigmentosa called cone-rod dystrophy, a rare and incurable disease. As I write this, she has very limited vision. When she looks at you, she turns her head 90 degrees and catches you out of the corner of her eyes. There's a chance the disease could stabilize and she could have limited vision forever. Hopefully, they'll find a cure within the next few years.

There's also a good chance she might lose her eyesight completely.

I am so scared of Rebecca's going blind that I make jokes about it. Not jokes in the stand-up comedy sense, but we find ways to laugh about it. She will pretend to see things I know she can't. She gets a kick out of being able to listen in on any conversation since her hearing has compensated for her eyesight; she's a human wiretap. We have a tandem bicycle and I'll tell her to take the lead. When she bumps into something, she's the first one with a wisecrack.

I've spent the better part of 11 chapters talking about how Fun Is Good applies in the workplace. Yet that matters little if it's not something you apply in all aspects of your life, especially at home. You can't turn it on and off; it has to be something that permeates every element of your existence—even in dealing with adversity.

When Rebecca was first diagnosed, I struggled with how to deal with her. Thankfully, I had my old man to draw upon for inspiration. He already had been gone for more than a decade, but he left behind a blueprint.

Rebecca knew all the stories about the exploding scoreboard, the midget Eddie Gaedel, Larry Doby, and planting ivy on the walls of Wrigley Field. Now I told her about how Dad made people comfortable with his having just one leg. He was never disabled or handicapped, just "crippled," and he did not let that slow him down.

I told her about how he poked fun at himself. About how he would gather all the neighborhood kids around him and then drive a nail through his wooden knee and tell them to go home and ask their fathers to do the same. About how each spring he would paint his wooden leg bronze and then spend the rest of the year trying to tan his body to match. About how his kids, especially me, would hide his wooden leg from him.

Laughing about horrible things makes them manageable. We're so fearful of the unknown and potential failure, but if you take the fear out, throw it on the table, play with it, and laugh about it, it makes it all seem surmountable.

Like Dad, I've never turned down a chance to speak to a charitable organization, and I thank God for that. Otherwise, I'd feel like a hypocrite.

No matter how successful you are, there might come a time when you're going to need some charitable help, if not financially, then at least for information, guidance, and support.

We've heard from parents who have gone through retinitis pigmentosa with their children. Others have sent holy water, candles from shrines, prayer cards, letters of support—anything they thought might help. One father gave me some good advice, explaining how his daughter loved to ride in boats because the sensation of the wind in her hair gave her back part of the freedom she had lost. No wonder Rebecca loves horseback riding and convertibles.

We quickly learned that there's a whole world dealing with problems like Rebecca's, and it's not a point of weakness to seek out help. Life is a series of sad events, so let's be up-front about it and take an extra moment to take the pulse of the people around us, especially at work. You never know what challenges they're facing. The successful people are the ones who show this empathy.

We've received all kinds of support from various foundations associated with retinitis pigmentosa, and we're extremely grateful. I'm able to accept such support with a clear conscience because I've made it a point to get involved with charities through the years, following Dad's advice that it's not just the right thing to do but is also good business.

Here too, the Fun Is Good philosophy applies. In 1990, I went out on a limb and hired a man by the name of Don Wardlow to serve as a radio analyst for the Miami Miracle. Over the years, Wardlow worked for several of our teams and once did a few innings of work for the Florida Marlins.

Don Wardlow is blind, but this is not a case of charity or cheap theatrics. Sure, it generated some publicity, but Wardlow is a gifted broadcaster. As his play-by-play partner calls the game, Don chimes in with analysis perfectly timed between pitches. You'd never know he was blind by listening to him. He can paint a detailed picture over the radio better than most announcers with 20/20 vision. Early in Don's career, we began including scorecards in our programs written in Braille.

Some might say Rebecca's diagnosis is an especially cruel karmic twist. Several journalists have written that I should be the last one to have a daughter go blind.

But I don't feel sorry for myself, not when it's Rebecca facing the disease. Plus, Rebecca won't let you feel sorry for her. In that way, she's just like my dad, who refused to admit he was handicapped—just crippled.

Not long after Rebecca was diagnosed, she and I developed the "R.P. song."

"Retinitis," she would sing.

"Pigmentosa," I would croon back.

Rebecca will bump into things on purpose just to get a few laughs, though of course she sometimes does so unintentionally. There's nothing funny about retinitis pigmentosa, of course, but laughter is the only way I know how to deal with things.

I'm not going to say there's a silver lining in any of this. There's no upside or good that's come about, though we're happy that the Veeck name and Rebecca's willingness to talk to the media has drawn attention to the disease and hopefully helped expedite the search for a cure.

I've learned so many things from Rebecca. The day she was diagnosed with R.P., she and Libby walked out of the hospital and saw an 8-year-old girl sitting in a wagon with a pump in her hands. Her father said she had just undergone her third open-heart surgery.

Regardless of your religious affiliation—or lack thereof—you have to admit that life has an uncanny ability to provide the proper perspective.

When Rebecca was diagnosed, we figured we would have to show her how to deal with this disease. In fact, it's been quite the opposite. She has shown us and others how to handle it. Rebecca embodies every element of Fun Is Good, to the point where it's valuable to take a look at the philosophy through the eyes of a child.

Rebecca may have poor eyesight, but she possesses tremendous vision. A few years ago, we were having a family dinner out with some friends. Rebecca asked to be excused and walked over to a nearby table, where a man was sitting by himself.

She was just far enough away that we could not hear the conversation, and I suppose we should have been a bit concerned when the chat continued for 15 minutes. Given her outgoing personality, I figured she must have known the man.

"Who was that, Rebecca?" I asked when she returned.

"Just someone who looked a little lonely," she said. "I thought he needed someone to talk to."

I looked over to the table and the man was wiping away a tear, as was one of our dinner companions.

I'm not sure where she gets this instinct. Her other senses compensate for a lack of eyesight, but it's as if her terrible affliction has given her a sixth sense of knowing what's going on with people. We talked about the "human touch" in Chapter Four. Most of us fail to take an interest in others when it's obvious there's something wrong. We've become so wrapped up in our lives and thoughts that we don't take the time to listen to other people or even notice how they're doing.

Even with limited eyesight, Rebecca can spot troubled folks from across the room.

She has the perfect attitude and perspective, those two valuable workplace skills discussed in Chapter Two. We're a nation of whiners, especially in corporate America, but Rebecca rarely complains about her predicament. She might melt down once or twice a year; it's remarkable that it doesn't happen more often.

I can't think of anything scarier than the possibility of waking up one morning without eyesight. Any challenge or setback at the office pales in comparison. The next time you're dealing with something at work, think of that person down the hall struggling with cancer, a death in the family, or a child with muscular dystrophy.

If you don't have someone like this in your life, go to a hospital and get to know somebody. You'll be amazed at how these people inspire and how it will help you in the workplace.

Focus on how they're dealing with *real* problems, and it sure does lighten your load. How dare we whine? Every day I ask how I'd deal with a situation if I were losing my eyesight. Suddenly I feel invincible, especially when I see how Rebecca handles things.

I used to get annoyed by airport delays and minor inconveniences. Most of us spend lifetimes trying unsuccessfully to develop patience and tolerance. Yet Rebecca takes things in stride even though she has a built-in reason to complain.

Rebecca could have written the chapter on irreverence. She has the dry, acerbic wit of a much older person. When we're in New York, she'll inevitably walk into a parking meter or fire hydrant and make fun of herself.

Her playfulness comes out constantly. A few years ago, we were asked to appear on *The View*, the morning talk show on ABC hosted by Barbara Walters, Meredith Vieira, and Star Jones. We got there a few hours early and settled into the green room. Edie Falco, the actress from *The Sopranos,* was there with a few of her people.

Every half hour, a producer would come in and go over the questions the hosts were going to ask Rebecca. Obviously, they wanted no surprises from a 9-year-old.

During the third round of preinterviewing, Rebecca was a little smart-alecky, at least by the standards of her usually perfect manners.

I was upset. "Rebecca, you will not be rude."

She nodded at Edie Falco. "Not one person has asked her what she's going to say. It's because I'm a kid."

Finally, we were led onstage. Rebecca took my hand and winked. "Dad, let's change all the answers and just have some fun."

"I'm with you, honey."

Rebecca spoke from the heart. She was articulate, funny, and everything they didn't expect from a 9-year-old. We even sang the "R.P. Song" for them. The hosts and audience loved her. As we left, the producers high-fived her and said she was a natural.

"Yeah, right," she said under her breath. She understood, as adults would, that the comments, while sincere, were condescending.

Look, you can't blame the producers. How many 9-year-olds are that articulate? But it pointed out to me that we don't look at children as individuals. We assume they won't be able to handle things. That's not the philosophy we take in our organization, where we walk a fine line with child labor laws on what we allow kids to do. Youth, as we've discussed, is vital to any company.

Rebecca knew how to handle an interview and wasn't going to embarrass herself. I was approaching 40 before I could go onstage without coming across as a bumbling fool. Rebecca just talks from the heart, even though she can't see the audience.

We saw another instance of this a couple of years ago in St. Paul. A group of fans in Section F—the "Section F'ers"—take up a collection whenever a player hits a home run. It harkens back to the tradition where fans gave the till to the batter.

The Saints fans collected money over the course of the season and by the end of the year had about $5,000, which they decided to donate to the Foundation Fighting Blindness. On the last day of the season, Rebecca was called up to the public address announcer's booth to accept the check on behalf of the foundation.

She thanked the fans profusely and spoke about how important it is that little children never be subjected to this disease. She talked about how it was going to help others, not her. Without realizing it, she's become a warrior and spokesperson for others.

Little kids gravitate to her and already she's a mentor. Several friends have called her wise beyond her years. She babysits, and parents are comfortable leaving children with her. She doesn't let kids get too far away, and she always can see them. The children don't know there's anything wrong with her, and they're instantly attracted to this gentle soul.

Like Dad, Rebecca puts people at ease with her ailment. That doesn't mean it's easy for her. Junior high is a difficult period for anyone, let alone someone who can't see very well. Some kids will sneak up from behind and push her. They'll wet down bathroom floors so she'll fall. Talk about cruel.

Yet we found out about these things only when teachers mentioned it to us at parent-teacher conferences. When we brought it up to Rebecca, she said there wasn't any problem. She could deal with problems on her own—and has. I pity the kid who pushes her from behind and incurs her verbal wrath. She can punch in the direction of voices, which she can pick out better than those with perfect sight.

Some teachers remarked that Rebecca is a little aggressive. You bet she is. Would you rather have somebody who is reticent so that kids will walk all over her? Rebecca is a survivor.

Everyone went to school with some person who was picked on relentlessly. At the time, it made you feel superior, though you're haunted by your petty actions later. That kid takes the abuse, and we have to live with it. All we had to do was to defend that person and take some of the blows instead of piling on the insults. It shouldn't be that difficult.

The same thing happens in the workplace. If you take those people who are a little strange under your wing and try to figure out what they're dealing with, the company will be better off. You'll become even more indispensable to the business.

Because of what Rebecca has faced, she does a tremendous job providing customer service when she answers phones and deals with people who wander into the office. She understands that taking extra time with a customer is important. Each person has a story or a situation and needs time to explain it. She takes the time to listen.

Why don't we take that extra 2 minutes to talk to people? When it comes to effective time management, good customer service companies probably get low ratings. But quality customer service doesn't run on the clock. It runs on heart.

Rebecca has ambitions to perform on Broadway. After that, she wants to become a fourth-generation baseball operator. I have no doubt she'll succeed in whatever she pursues, though I wouldn't be surprised if she ends up doing work for a nonprofit entity that involves caring for others. After all, she's been both the victim of a horrible disease and the recipient of kindness. She's seen it from all sides. At the age of 13, she's a powerful public speaker. I can't wait to see what good transpires when she channels her passions toward specific goals.

She very well might devote her life to other people, mentoring and volunteering. That's not just customer service: It's the ultimate in service.

As for "Lessons from Dad," Rebecca has rewritten the book.

It's funny how life repeats itself. Not long after her illness was diagnosed, I dusted off Dad's old lines and gags. To put her at ease, I told her all the stories about how he dealt with having just one leg. He made having a peg leg seem swashbuckling, and he never ducked questions about it. That made people comfortable, especially kids.

When they saw a one-legged man doing laps in the pool, it didn't seem like a big deal. It was just that silly Bill Veeck. Dad never complained about his lot in life, and it was entirely genuine. He didn't turn it on for the public and take out his frustrations at home.

I've never believed in reincarnation, but I've been giving it some careful consideration because of Rebecca. Like Dad, she's blue-eyed and blonde, fair-skinned and left-handed. If you look at her from the nose up, the resemblance is eerie. Like Dad, she's a wonderful dancer, which lends credence to the notion that some talents skip a generation. She has endless curiosity and varied interests, including piano, dance, writing, horseback riding, and karate.

Like Dad, she puts people who might not know how to handle her ailment at ease. Like Dad, she loves reading, though for her it takes the form of books on tape. I told her there are 250 classics everyone should read in their lifetime. She'll have the list finished by the time she enters high school.

Like Dad, she loves to laugh and has one chuckle that starts deep in her solar plexus and just warms your heart. She understands that she is a nonsighted person in a world of sight, but she's not averse to throwing out self-deprecating lines.

"Not a bad throw for a blind kid," she'll say.

It's not meant to solicit sympathy or even a response. It's just her way of dealing with it. You'd think there would be more anger or resentment, but somehow she manages to channel it into something else. I'll never know how she internalizes it.

For most people, the way to deal with something as tragic as a death in the family or divorce is to become immersed in work. It's the easiest way to take the mind off things. I don't know how Rebecca deals with her loss of sight, but it's inspiring.

Not surprisingly, members of the media often want to talk with her. Libby and I leave it up to Rebecca, who almost always agrees to sit for interviews and answer the same questions over and over in order to draw attention to the fight against blindness. Her only condition is that she be interviewed alone, unless of course the news outlet wants to hear my tired shtick as part of the story.

Early in each interview, she'll mention that her loss of eyesight bothers her parents more than it does her. We recently took her for her annual eye exam, and the doctor told her things had not gotten any worse, which is encouraging.

But there have been other times when the news has not been so good. From my perspective, her eyesight is not very good. But she'll say it's not that bad and that she just has some gray spots in her eyes.

The doctor even asks her for help. "You're going to have to help put your parents at ease," he told her once.

Rebecca will be in the seventh grade when this book is published. She already knows how to handle adults better than adults do. A few years ago, she went door to door selling wrapping paper. In the absence of adequate budgets, this is how schools raise money in the twenty-first century.

She went to visit a lady in our neighborhood, a woman whom I had not managed to meet, despite my good efforts. When the woman answered the door, Rebecca gave a 20-second sales pitch and sort of turned away.

"Why don't you look at me when you're speaking?" the woman huffed.

"I have an eye disease," Rebecca replied, matter-of-factly. "I *am* looking at you."

When I heard what happened I wanted to storm over and give that woman an earful. How could she be so rude and presumptuous?

Rebecca stopped me. "I don't need you to fight my battles," she said. "I'll deal with it."

And so she has. I can't think of anything scarier than retinitis pigmentosa. This is Rebecca's reality. But she sleeps well because she knows she'll be able to deal with it.

So the next time you're overwhelmed at work, feeling too busy to chat with coworkers and customers, or so stressed that you're unable to laugh or enjoy life, think of the Rebeccas of the world who manage to thrive under far greater pressures.

When my coauthor and I first came up with the idea for this book, just a few months after Rebecca was diagnosed, we had a difficult time focusing on the message. Over the next few years, this magical little girl with limited eyesight unwittingly helped us shape the Fun Is Good vision in the most appropriate way possible.

Through the eyes of a child.

. . . .

Fun Is Good Vignette

Rebecca Veeck

"I don't care anymore if I go blind. I'd rather it not happen, of course, but I'll deal with it. Sometimes I feel like God doesn't listen or isn't there. But I believe in Him and feel that there's some reason behind this."

Sometimes I get upset because I won't be able to drive. I can't read books and that stinks. I used to be able to read an entire book in 2 days. Now I watch my parents read or go online and it's frustrating.

But I don't let it slow me down. I like to dance, play piano, ride horses, and swim. I can read books—on tape—sometimes getting through an 800-page book in a day. I go to the ballparks and have fun. I can still have as much fun as I want. I see people, especially adults, who have perfect eyesight and don't seem capable of having fun. That's sad.

It seems like some people have forgotten how to have fun. They do things for money, not for the fun of it. These people even have a hard time having fun at ballparks, where it's impossible not to enjoy yourself.

It's the same thing when it comes to dealing with customers. People behind the front desk should be ecstatic to help customers. Instead, they often give off an air of "What do you want?" You don't need perfect eyesight to see the difference.

I'm extremely lucky to have grown up learning to deal with adversity by looking for the fun in life. For me, the basic idea is that if you don't think you're going to have fun, you won't, and you end up having an air of sadness and depression that pulls you and everyone around you down.

If I didn't keep myself busy, I don't know how sad I'd be. I have to try twice as hard as the other students at my school to get the same grades and I'm okay with that. It's when I'm easy on myself or feel sorry for myself that things start slipping out of control. I imagine it's that way for everyone.

Fun Is Good because that's the way life is supposed to be. It's the main feeling that we're supposed to have. I mean, if you're not having fun, what's the point?

• •

FUN IS GOOD

Chapter 12 Summary and Exercises (Through the Eyes of a Child)

- Get to know someone confined to a hospital bed. You'll be amazed at how such people inspire you, especially in the workplace.
- No matter how bad you think things are going, remember that someone else has it worse.
- If people can remain upbeat despite the loss of eyesight, it shouldn't be difficult for those of us with normal vision to maintain a positive attitude.
- Always look for ways to laugh at adversity.

Afterword

· ·

The Fun Is Good Challenge

MY GREATEST GIFT is that I'm able to point people in the right direction. I can take a look at their skills, personality, and mindset and know where they can best find joy and passion in their workplace and career.

I don't have the benefit of that one-on-one interaction here, but I hope you'll be able to use this book as a blueprint to find that fulfillment in your career and life.

You've read all of these anecdotes of my life and how you can apply them to your career and business, whether you own and operate one or simply are a cog in the wheel. Too often, we read books and find information both motivating and entertaining but never apply it.

We began this book with the notion that there is no fun in the workplace. Most people sleepwalk through careers that aren't compelling, and they're not fulfilling their potential. They have no fun at work, they take those frustrations home, and over time they lose any passion they ever had for anything.

The real test of this book is whether you'll take these ideas and apply them. I want you to go back to each of the summaries at the ends of the chapters and take them to your workplace. See what works and what does not. Find out what the acceptance rate is from your coworkers, bosses, or employees. Let us know what's effective, what isn't, what is not applicable, and what leads to conflict.

This book should lessen conflict as it defines the workplace in terms of being more fun and productive. Still, there might be elements of Fun Is Good that don't work in your situation. I understand that. After all, I had a difficult time bringing about sweeping Fun Is Good change in Major League Baseball. But you'll find that most (if not all) of Fun Is Good can apply to your workplace and your career.

Throughout the book, I've talked about companies that have used the philosophies found here in Fun Is Good to achieve success. I don't believe for a minute that the people who run companies like Southwest Airlines, Ritz-Carlton, Costco, and Hormel Foods (SPAM) even know who I am, let alone are in any way inspired by my work.

On the other hand, you've heard from leaders of Outback Steakhouse, Hooters Restaurants, and Gallery Furniture who have applied these same principles successfully. The bottom line is that those companies that hire passionate people, promote a workplace where ideas and irreverence are valued, nurture change and careers, and place a premium on customer service are the ones that will be successful.

And it can all be fun.

The idea that companies must provide superior customer service and give their employees a fun, nurturing workplace is gaining strength throughout corporate America. The businesses that can do both will be the ones that survive for the next 50 years.

I hope you'll take the lessons and exercises we've discussed in this book and apply them to your own career, whether you run a business, want to inject some Fun Is Good into your company as an employee, or simply wish to reposition your career goals.

I've had great success supporting people in pursuit of careers where they can best apply their talents and find professional fulfillment by working in an atmosphere in which Fun Is Good thrives. Many of them have moved beyond minor league baseball and sports and have brought Fun Is Good to other industries. I couldn't be happier.

I've worked for a lot of businesses, from baseball to advertising to jai alai, and I've always been much more successful when I've had fun. I've learned more, been more productive, mentored more, and benefited more from mentoring.

The key to any business is to build as much fun into it as you possibly can. When the fun goes, the product fails. It's tougher for workers to get out of bed. Self-motivation and ambition fall by the wayside. Without fun in the workplace, we'll become less competitive as a nation and will be surpassed by other countries in the marketplace.

In order to keep people invigorated and stimulated, we have to speak to their inner core, and we're all in pursuit of joy. So why does that stop at work? Why do we have weekends that we look forward to voraciously and hobbies that we can't wait to lose ourselves in for a scant 12 hours over the weekend after torturing ourselves in the workplace for 40 to 80 hours? It doesn't make any sense. We should be in the pursuit of fun because it makes us more productive and makes businesses more successful.

It helps if Fun Is Good begins at the top with the chiefs embracing it, but if not, it can be a grassroots effort starting with one employee. If employees are determined to have fun, they will. It doesn't thwart teamwork. You can be the one voice of sanity saying, "I'm going to have fun no matter what you guys do." More often than not, people will defect to your side. It's a natural inclination and hardly a revolutionary step, not in today's workplace where people move constantly.

Now more than ever, you need to give this a shot because the old systems aren't there anymore. You're not going to receive the gold watch and pension, so why stick with a job that's not only insecure but no fun?

Remember, there's not a single field where Fun Is Good does not apply. In Chapter 7, we applied the promotional touch to all manner of businesses; if you're still stumped for how it could work for your line of work, drop me a line.

I hope you'll share with me your experiences applying Fun Is Good to your business, job, career, and life. No matter how small the progress, please let me know. You don't have to transform an entire industry or even your office. Maybe it's something as simple as not taking yourself too seriously, which helps you project a better attitude, which in turn leads to career growth. Maybe you created a more kid-friendly workplace or applied the human touch in a way that showed coworkers you cared.

If you made sweeping changes, I'd like to hear about them as well. Did you overhaul your customer service? Did you knock down walls and take doors off meeting rooms to better foster communication and rid the workplace of office paranoia?

Did you implement something whimsical and irreverent that made your coworkers and customers laugh? Did you take stock of your passions and reposition your career to better match your passions?

Whatever you do with Fun Is Good, please share your stories with me at mike@funisgood.net. Tell me how it has transformed your life—and not just in the workplace. I want to know how it's helped you create a more fulfilling life overall.

We'll pick the most inspirational submissions and, at the very least, post them on funisgood.net. Perhaps we'll be so moved to bring you to speak at or attend our Veeck Promotional seminar. You can share with me in person how you applied Fun Is Good to bring joy and passion into your workplace and career.

I look forward to hearing from you.

—Mike Veeck

About The Authors

MIKE VEECK is recognized as one of the leading experts on customer service, promotions, and fun in the workplace. As the co-owner of six minor league baseball teams, he's made a career of trying what other people wouldn't dare. Promotions such as Nobody Night, Mime-O-Vision, and Vasectomy Night have attracted national attention and brought fun back to the ballpark. A veteran advertising professional, marketing consultant, keynote speaker, and founder of the Veeck Promotional Seminar, Mike has carried on the legacy of his father Bill Veeck, the late maverick promoter and Hall of Fame baseball owner.

The younger Veeck and his teams have developed a reputation for unparalleled customer service, and Mike has proven that his strategies are not specific to baseball. He has appeared on or been profiled by numerous media outlets, including *60 Minutes,* HBO's *Real Sports,* the *NBC Nightly News,* ABC's *Nightline,* CBS *Sunday Morning* news, National Public Radio, *Fortune Small Business* magazine, *ESPN the Magazine, SportsBusiness Journal,* and *USA Today.* He's also been a central figure in three books written on the Northern League and his St. Paul Saints.

A graduate of Loyola College in Baltimore, Veeck began his baseball career working for the Chicago White Sox in 1975 as assistant business manager and director of marketing. After his infamous "Disco Demolition" promotion in 1979 and his father's sale of the White Sox, he spent a decade out of baseball working in advertising and promotions in South Florida. Those skills served him well when he returned to the game in 1990 to resurrect the Miami (now Fort Myers) Miracle, and later as he helped build the independent Northern League into an unlikely success story.

Veeck has worked for four Major League clubs: the White Sox, Tampa Bay Devil Rays, Florida Marlins, and Detroit Tigers. A gifted speaker, he has entertained companies such as 3M, General Mills, the NBA, and NASCAR. He has been the featured speaker for the American Bar Association and Newspaper Association of America and never misses an opportunity to speak to students at colleges and universities.

Veeck is a principal in the the Goldklang Group, the minor league baseball ownership contingent that includes actor Bill Murray, singer Jimmy Buffett, and Marv Goldklang, a limited partner of the New York Yankees. Veeck oversees the popular Veeck Seminar, a series of annual marketing-related conventions that teach the philosophies of Bill and Mike Veeck to professionals from throughout business.

Mike is married to Libby Veeck and has two children, William "Night Train" and Rebecca. They live in Mt. Pleasant, South Carolina.

PETE WILLIAMS is a contributing writer to *Street & Smith's SportsBusiness Journal.* He has written about sports, business, and fitness for numerous publications, including *USA Today* and the *Washington Post,* and is the author of two books on the sports memorabilia business: *Card Sharks* and *Sports Memorabilia for Dummies.* He teamed with trainer and sports performance expert Mark Verstegen to write *Core Performance,* published by Rodale in 2004. A graduate of the University of Virginia, Williams lives in Safety Harbor, Florida, with his wife, Suzy, and son, Luke.

For further information on Fun Is Good, please visit www.funisgood.net.

For further information on the Veeck Promotional Seminar, please visit www.veeckseminar.com.

For further information on Mike Veeck's minor league teams and other endeavors, please visit www.mikeveeck.com and www.goldklanggroup.com.

For information on the Fun Is Good corporate training video and teaching program, please visit www.starthrower.com or www.crmlearning.com.

For further information on Pete Williams, please visit www. petewilliams.net.

Index

. . . .

<u>Underscored</u> references indicate boxed text.

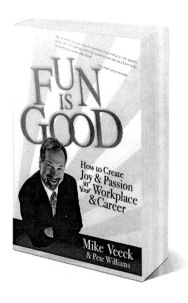

How can you use this book?

MOTIVATE

EDUCATE

THANK

INSPIRE

PROMOTE

CONNECT

Why have a custom version of *Fun Is Good*?

- Build personal bonds with customers, prospects, employees, donors, and key constituencies
- Develop a long-lasting reminder of your event, milestone, or celebration
- Provide a keepsake that inspires change in behavior and change in lives
- Deliver the ultimate "thank you" gift that remains on coffee tables and bookshelves
- Generate the "wow" factor

Books are thoughtful gifts that provide a genuine sentiment that other promotional items cannot express. They promote employee discussions and interaction, reinforce an event's meaning or location, and they make a lasting impression. Use your book to say "Thank You" and show people that you care.

Fun Is Good is available in bulk quantities and in customized versions at special discounts for corporate, institutional, and educational purposes. To learn more please contact our Special Sales team at:

1.866.775.1696 • sales@advantageww.com • www.AdvantageSpecialSales.com

CPSIA information can be obtained
at www.ICGtesting.com
Printed in the USA
FFOW04n1832060218
44934416-45172FF